HER SECRET & EXTRAORDINARY LIVES

Helen O'Neill

Hardie Grant Books

First published in 2006
Reprinted in 2006 (twice), 2007
by Hardie Grant Books
85 High Street
Prahran, Victoria 3181, Australia
www.hardiegrant.com.au

National Library of Australia Cataloguing-in-Publication Data:

O'Neill, Helen.
Florence Broadhurst : her secret and extraordinary lives
Includes index.
ISBN 978 1 74066 294 9.
ISBN 1 74066 294 6.
1. Broadhurst, Florence, 1899–1977. 2. Artists, Australian – Biography.
3. Businesswomen – Australia – Biography. I. Title.

700.92

Designed by Trisha Garner
Set in Adobe Caslon Pro & Bauer Bodoni
Cover image Floral 300 courtesy Signature Prints
Endpapers photograph: Collection, Powerhouse Museum, Sydney
Printed and bound in China by SNP Leefung

10 9 8 7 6 5 4

Contents

Preface

There is a fantastic lightness of being about Florence Broadhurst – about the lives she led, the loves she turned her back on and the legacies she left.

The most striking of those legacies is the Florence Broadhurst design library, an extraordinary collection of 530 hand-drawn patterns that originally made their mark in Australia as expensive, hand-printed, silk-screen wallpapers.

At first glance, the artistic and stylistic range of these patterns is astounding. They bound from intricate English tapestries to boastfully abstract geometrics, romantic florals, psychedelic pop art, dynamic orientals and witty, cartoon-like line drawings.

Of the entire range, one of the most arresting, stand-alone images is the luminous, utopian creation *Exotic Birds*. What makes *Exotic Birds* remarkable is not its size, although at almost a metre from tip to feathered tail the design dwarfs most of the other Broadhurst creations. It is that this artful, apparently simple image is created by pressing paint through five handcrafted silk-screens. Taken out of context,

'She was a bright flame of a woman who flared up and then vanished; a person you'd never forget,' says friend Barry Little of Broadhurst, photographed in 1926 in a painstakingly embroidered Mantón de Manilla, or Chinese shawl [opposite].

the pattern held on each of these five screens means nothing – a series of sweeping abstract, art deco curves sits on one; artfully drawn petals floating precariously in mid-air make up another; a third holds seamless, dynamic strokes that frustratingly leave skeletal outlines rather than any real guide as to what the finished image will be. Only when the five seemingly unrelated silk-screens are brought together, when layers of different-coloured inks are accurately applied through each, will the complete picture emerge.

This portrait of Florence Broadhurst takes the same approach; perhaps the only one possible with a woman who lived as she did, inventing different lives on different continents, tailoring her name and her history for each one. She carved her own bold passage through an era of enormous social upheaval, stepping into each new life as though it was a new theatrical role. She employed a different regimen of hair, make-up and clothing for each one. As the photographs from her family's archives show, Florence Broadhurst quite literally changed with the times.

VIII   *Exotic Birds [opposite].*
         COURTESY SIGNATURE PRINTS

At the age of sixty, following a series of secret lives, Florence Broadhurst declared that Australia was afraid of colour and publicly launched herself as a designer. She founded a high-class, hand-print wallpaper design studio in Sydney and over the following two decades became outrageously prolific, producing images that found their way from Australia to London, New York and Saudi Arabia.

On 15 October 1977, the creative hurricane suddenly came to an end when Florence Broadhurst was murdered in her Paddington wallpaper showroom. The attack was ferocious and brutal, her fingers broken and her body battered. At first glance, the motive appeared to be robbery. In the months that followed Florence Broadhurst's death, homicide detectives sifted through evidence, witness statements, rumour and hearsay in an abortive attempt to solve the crime. As the years brushed by, Florence Broadhurst's family and friends slowly emerged from the nightmarish horror of her murder and the police investigation that

came with it, some more wounded than others by the knowledge that until her killer was convicted, no one could really trust any of the others again. Wild stories spread of her supposed links with figures from the criminal underworld.

In the wider world, fashion moved on. Florence Broadhurst's flamboyant, sometimes retina-crunching panorama of patterns faded from view as walls were scraped clean, painted over and re-covered. Her entire archive, described by some as the Australian equivalent of that created by Britain's master patterner William Morris, was almost destroyed during a series of business takeovers in which the collection was not considered an asset worth keeping. She herself was remembered, if at all, as an outspoken, outlandish character from a bygone age who had inexplicably come to a terrible end.

I first heard the Florence Broadhurst story from Sue Clothier, a Sydney-based television producer, who invited me out for a drink in October 2003. She, Nicola Lawrence and Tim Toni had written up a documentary proposal about Florence Broadhurst, and Sue wondered whether I might be interested in meeting Florence's only son, Robert Lloyd-Lewis, with a view to writing a book.

That meeting – which took place in an intimate Italian restaurant in the Sydney suburb of Paddington not far from where Florence Broadhurst had worked and died – was a remarkable one. It was organised by Helen and David Lennie, the dynamic owners of Signature Prints, who were re-creating Florence Broadhurst's designs in earnest for the first time since her death, using the same time-consuming, hands-on craftsmanship that she had employed. Also present was Anne-Marie Van de Ven, curator of Decorative Arts and Design at Sydney's Powerhouse Museum, who was spearheading the development of a Broadhurst collection at the Powerhouse and who was fascinated by what little she then knew of Broadhurst's life.

Florence Broadhurst   XI
remained glamorous
well into her seventies,
as this portrait, taken
circa 1974, shows.
COURTESY ROBERT LLOYD–LEWIS

The guest of honour was Robert Lloyd-Lewis, who is now in his sixties. He and his vivacious wife Annie had travelled south from their home in mid-north Queensland to attend this meeting. Until that day, Lloyd-Lewis had steadfastly refused to candidly discuss his mother's life with any journalist since her murder twenty-six years earlier. His silence was borne of grief and shock, and it ran so deep that when he first met Annie, it took him three years to tell her who his mother even was. Out of respect for Lloyd-Lewis, others close to Broadhurst also refused to speak out.

Lloyd-Lewis's decision to even entertain the idea of cooperating on a book about his mother had not been made lightly, but he told me that one of the main reasons he wanted to do so was because he felt his mother deserved the recognition. Lloyd-Lewis is a solid, muscular man with a forthright attitude and with a career in transport and property development behind him – yet his nervousness was almost palpable – as was the fact that, despite it, he clearly wanted to talk about his mother and about how wounded he still was by the events surrounding her death. 'I need to know who killed her,' he told me during that very first meeting. 'I really need to know.'

*In **Ikeda** [opposite], Broadhurst created a clean, stylised, repetitive pattern of two-dimensional fans.*
COURTESY SIGNATURE PRINTS

Florence Broadhust and the spectacular design range she left behind have always provoked strong reactions. Akira Isogawa, one of Australia's top fashion designers, is a Broadhurst devotee who describes her as an inspiration. He was taken aback by the beauty of the handpainted designs from which the silk-screens are made when he saw them for the first time. 'I thought it was an artist's work,' he told me. 'I never thought it was already commercialised. It looked completely pure.'

To Anne-Marie Van de Ven, the Broadhurst design library is a rich, highly significant bank of creativity. It is part of a 'very, very important Australian archive,' she says. 'However,' she adds, 'one of the most important questions about it is exactly who created it.' Florence Broadhurst's eyesight was so bad by the end of her life that she could barely read a menu. Is it credible that she should seriously have claimed responsibility for such an enormous artistic output?

At least one of Broadhurst's acquaintances, designer Peter Travis, is in no doubt. Travis argues that her final and most successful theatrical performance – that of a great designer – was just that: an act. 'She was an opportunistic con-woman,' he told me without compunction. 'A good confidence trickster.'

The truth of this matter – like many of the so-called truths relating to Florence Broadhurst – is not so simple. Reaching into her past has involved approaching everybody from the titled wives of former Australian prime ministers to international touring stars, convicted criminals, printers, artists, gallery owners, journalists, detectives and even a brothel owner. It has necessitated travelling as far afield as Mount Perry, the place of Broadhurst's birth – a remote, drought-prone patch of Queensland – to visit the house her family grew up in and the tiny rural community she left behind, and also her stomping grounds in England.

I have dived into libraries in the northern and southern hemispheres to get to the bottom of some of Broadhurst's secrets – such as exactly who was the husband she hid from her family and friends – and have felt the frustration of trying to establish whether past events Broadhurst claimed as facts really happened. Proving somebody did something is relatively easy. Proving they did not can be surprisingly hard.

One unassailable fact is that Florence Broadhurst delighted in making a scene. In her final incarnation, she did this in a literal sense, creating a design studio which produced the impressive array of images featured in this book. Some of these patterns are staggeringly beautiful, yet the questions they provoke are more stunning still.

Is Florence Broadhurst the designer who created this work? If not, who is? Why have they never come forward? Why did she swathe so much of her life in secrecy, even from her own family? Why was

*Broadhurst's take on the mythical bird **Phoenix** is executed here in blue ink on white paper.*
COURTESY SIGNATURE PRINTS

she murdered? Did her friendship with John Glover, the serial killer who would later become known as the Granny Killer, have anything to do with it?

After Florence Broadhurst's death, Robert Lloyd-Lewis needed some answers. He flew from his Queensland home to the south coast of England to visit an old friend of his mother's, an elderly woman he had always known as 'Aunt Dorothy', even though, in truth, they were not related.

The bond between Dorothy and Florence Broadhurst was a strange one. For decades, Broadhurst paid an allowance to Dorothy transferring money every month from Australian dollars to English pounds to make Dorothy's life that little bit easier. It marked an obligation dating back from before Robert Lloyd-Lewis's birth and he had no idea what it meant.

When Broadhurst died, Lloyd-Lewis phoned Dorothy to tell her that he would continue the payments. Dorothy cried. Then he went to visit her in the nursing home she lived in near Brighton. Lloyd-Lewis sat down with the gentle, white-haired woman and asked her, 'Please. Please tell me about my mother.'

'Robert,' she replied. 'You have no idea who your mother really was.'

chapter one

Stepping onto the stage

Florence Broadhurst first opened her large grey eyes on 28 July 1899, but not in the aristocratic English surroundings to which she would later lay claim. Despite the fantastic tales that this bold, dynamic, relentless performer later wove into her constantly changing life history, Florence Broadhurst's first entrance occurred with little fanfare and less luxury in an unprepossessing corner of one of the great cattle stations of south-east Queensland.

Her birth took place in pioneer country, fifty years after the European explorers who laid claim to Australia started running livestock across the vast, inhospitable landscape. Her thirty-year-old father, Bill, managed one of the oldest properties – a 300 000 acre wilderness called Mungy Station – but the Broadhursts themselves owned nothing. They lived in a simple workers' cottage: a small, wood-built, tin-roofed shack with a wood-burning stove.

Mount Perry, the nearest town, had a population of 250. Visiting the town meant negotiating a twenty-mile path that was little more than a goat track. Families as isolated as the Broadhursts grew their own

Japanese Bamboo [opposite] reflects the English take on chinoiserie evident in the early 1900s. Its appeal lies squarely in its boldness.

COURTESY SIGNATURE PRINTS

vegetables, made their own bread and killed their own whiptails – the local wallabies – for meat. No refrigeration meant fresh flesh for two days at most. After that, it was salt meat until the next kill.

Florence Broadhurst's parents, the two personalities who shaped her earliest days, appeared to be polar opposites. Her mother, Margaret Ann, is remembered as a quiet, diligent soul who had her work cut out for her. Managing stock and a team of drovers took her husband deep into the bush where he would spend his weeks sleeping rough, so Margaret was often alone with their children: son Fassifern, who was three when Florence was born, and two-year-old daughter May Millicent. Another daughter, Maude, born eleven months before Florence's arrival, lived only twelve days and lies buried in a tiny, unmarked grave on Mungy Station. Young Florence was made of sterner stuff. She was very much her father's daughter.

Talk to those who knew William Broadhurst and a picture emerges of a muscular, tough, utterly single-minded individual who let nothing stand in his way. He came from English stock but was a pure Aussie larrikin whose first love was the land. One of thirteen children, he spent his youth droving other people's cattle through the raw expanse of Queensland's harsh pastures. He was known far and wide as being good with a bull whip, a horse, a gun, his wits and his fists.

In later years Bill Broadhurst became a local councillor. Ted Bettiens, an elderly blue-eyed cowboy, knew Broadhurst well. Bettiens still lives on the outskirts of Mount Perry in a little yellow house, and remembers his friend as quick-tongued and fiercely frugal, with a wicked sense of humour and an explosive temper. Council meetings that Broadhurst attended had a tendency to escalate into bare-knuckle brawls if things did not go his way, and he had no qualms about showing his impatience with those not as focused on the meetings as Broadhurst felt they should be. Bettiens was there the night that Broadhurst dropped a box of lit matches into the open mouth of a fellow council member who had unwisely fallen asleep during a meeting.

The skills Florence learnt at the Mount Perry tennis club came in handy in the racquet clubs of Paris in later years. Florence is second from the left.

4   *At sixteen, Florence looked every bit the demure young country lady. She is pictured here in 1915, seated middle front. Her sister Cilla is standing behind.*

The main thing Bettiens remembers about Bill Broadhurst is his unusual ability as a storyteller. The man, says Bettiens, was a master. He spun the most incredible spontaneous bush yarns with a face so straight that the fabrications would fool his listeners every time. It is no surprise to Bettiens that Bill Broadhurst's daughter Florence developed exactly the same skill.

By the time Florence's younger sister Priscilla appeared on the scene in September 1902, Bill had saved enough to buy a patch of the sunburnt landscape he loved so much. Near the tiny settlement of Drummers Creek, a few miles east of Mount Perry, he built 'The Oakes', the first Broadhurst family home. Here, as Florence grew, a patchwork pattern of seasons flashed past. Winter brought bone-bitingly cold weather. Summer heralded a searing sun and temperatures that hit the mid-thirties. Heavy rains flooded the valleys, cutting families off for weeks at a time.

In the nearby mining town of Mount Perry, fortunes rose and fell with the international price of copper. Before Florence was born, Mount Perry could boast only 200 inhabitants but by her eighth birthday, in 1907, the population had catapulted to 3675. Red-hot copper smelters lit up the night sky, pubs opened to cater for hordes of thirsty prospectors, and shops began touting temptations from the world beyond. Bill Broadhurst was not interested. He wanted more land and he made sure he got it, purchasing a large acreage called 'Elliotts Creek', south-west of Mount Perry, where he ran his own cattle.

Bill Broadhurst was more than a cattle farmer, though; he was a social pioneer. He wanted to forge a genteel society for his family and, as Florence and her siblings grew up, they became part of a new social class in this young, emerging nation: the landed gentry.

Family photographs show the Broadhurst girls as neat young ladies who are the image of demure, Victorian childhood. Dressed in their Sunday best for the camera, they play tennis – a lifelong love of their father's and a useful game to know in social circles – and go to picnics with nicely turned out young gentlemen. They learnt needlework – an essential skill for the homemaker – and Florence became adept at making her own dresses for dances and the other events on the social calendar. It was a skill that one of her future incarnations, the French couturier Madame Pellier, would find very useful indeed.

Florence's tiny school at Drummers Creek still exists. Today, it is a lonely building which sits seemingly abandoned in the middle of a field. A local landowner, whose ancestors once played tennis with the young Broadhursts, now uses it as a store for hay. This is where the Broadhurst siblings, from the early 1900s, began their education. Young ladies needed more than reading, writing and arithmetic, however, so Mrs Annie Dale, the sophisticated wife of Mount Perry's chemist, offered the Broadhurst sisters piano lessons. It immediately became clear that Florence was something special. She was quick to pick up keyboard skills and she could sing, in strong, clear contralto tones that demanded special attention.

On Saturday mornings, Florence's older sister May drove her in the family's horse-drawn buggy to Mount Perry where she caught a train to Bundaberg, sixty-six miles away, for personal singing lessons. As her confidence and skills grew, she began to give small recitals for her family and groups of friends. For the very first time, Florence realised the thrill of having an audience.

She was careful to keep newspaper cuttings of these first steps into the public arena. Her earliest notice, yellow with age and stored in Sydney's Mitchell Library, records her performance as a nineteen-year-old at the Grand Patriotic Concert, a fundraiser for soldiers held in Bundaberg on Wednesday 7 August 1918. She is listed as second after the interval, singing *Beyond the Dawn*. Promotion came fast. By Thursday 31 October 1918, in another fundraiser, she is second on the programme, with a rendition of *Still As the Night*.

In all the cuttings that Florence Broadhurst so carefully kept, there is a glaring omission. There is no newspaper notice – not even a dog-eared programme – of what should have been the proudest moment of an up-and-coming contralto's young life: the duet of *Abide With Me* that Broadhurst apparently performed with the international British singing star Dame Clara Butt after winning a local Eisteddford.

This is where the real fun in the hunt to find Florence begins. Is it conceivable that she did not keep a record of this momentous event? Is it possible that she lost whatever evidence there may have been? The difficulty is that her story changes as the years go by. Florence variously let it be known that she won the Eisteddford, that she came second, and that she was so good she could have toured with two luminaries of Australian performing history, singer Dame Nellie Melba and dancer Robert Helpmann, had fate in the form of injury not intervened.

6 *The geometric strength of Kabuki [opposite] lies in the sheer scale of the design.*

The man everybody believed to be Florence Broadhurst's husband, Leonard Lloyd Lewis, recounted yet another version of this story after her death, in which Dame Clara introduced a performance by the sixteen-year-old Broadhurst at Brisbane's Anglican Cathedral. In fact, Dame Clara toured Australia when Broadhurst was fifteen and again when she was twenty but the archive of St John's Anglican Cathedral in Brisbane has no record of either of them appearing there. Brisbane's other obvious venues also draw a blank.

Broadhurst's sister Priscilla, known to family and friends as Cilla, described the moment of Florence's appearance with Dame Clara in detail years later but was Cilla any more reliable than other members of the mischievous Broadhurst clan? I will come back to this later, and to the problems of sifting fact from fiction in the amazing technicolour tapestry that Florence Broadhurst wove around her history before she began creating images so bold that few thought to question anything beyond them.

What is clear is that young Florence Broadhurst's solo career did not take off. With a resilience that would become one of her trademarks, she moved straight on to plan B, auditioning for and securing a job with a touring theatre troupe headed by a manager determined to make his mark on the international scene. It was called the Smart Set Diggers.

This was a major break for Broadhurst and her ticket out of rural life. Her fellow cast members were dynamic, lively and quite unlike anybody she had met before. One was destined to became a lifelong friend – Ralph Sawyer, a Sydney-born female impersonator whose World War I life as an enlisted soldier had seen him do everything from stretcher duty at the battle of Gallipoli to performances in women's clothing as a member of the Anzac Coves (a soldier–entertainer troupe so popular they even gave a command performance for the British king and queen).

Back then, working as a female impersonator using exaggerated mannerisms and clothes to comic effect had nothing – overtly – to do with sexual identity. During World War I, some male soldiers simply made a speciality of it. Ralph Sawyer was just such a performer. He joined the Smart Set Diggers in 1920, when it was an all-male group of ex-soldiers. By the time Broadhurst came on board, probably in early 1922, their manager Richard Norton had a new vision. He renamed the eight-strong cast of musicians, female impersonators, singers and comedians the Globe Trotters and organised what would become a massive, fifteen-month tour of Asia. His troupe included singer Florence Broadhurst, comedians Richard Norton and Dick Crichton, female impersonators Charles Holt and Ralph Sawyer, and pianist Wallingford Tate, who would become a close friend to Broadhurst. Two other female performers – Leila Forbes and Dorothy Drew – began the tour but dropped out and were replaced before it finished.

On 4 December 1922, Florence Broadhurst left Brisbane on the 4072-ton steam ship *Montoro* bound for Singapore. She called herself 'Bobby Broadhurst' on the passenger manifest. This was the nickname the drag queens in the troupe had given her, Broadhurst later told her son,

Fingers [opposite] – an example of Broadhurst's confidence in eye-catching modernist design.

COURTESY SIGNATURE PRINTS

9

because when she joined as a forthright, self-confident 22-year-old, she 'became the male'.

The moniker stuck. It marks Florence Broadhurst's first true step into reinvention, a process that would involve drawing a line between her previous life and the one into which she was about to plunge. Florence came from a small country town far from anywhere. Bobby was an ingenue with the world at her feet. Florence was an attractive young woman of marriageable age who should have been looking for a well-to-do husband to father her children. Bobby was an independently minded minx, a symbol of a new era. Bobby was going places and, as she and her globe trotting colleagues watched Australia disappear from the stern of their ocean liner, they knew they had only a few weeks before their first performance – at the Dutch colony of Java, Bali, in late December. That sea voyage would have been a frantic whirl of rehearsal: improving the skits, practising quick changes from one flamboyant costume to another, and polishing song-and-dance routines.

A rare signed photograph of Bobby Broadhurst [opposite]. This portrait was taken in Hong Kong during the Globe Trotter's fifteen-month tour of Asia.

10

Broadhurst honed the art of creating Bobby with greasepaint, costume, movement and voice. She looked every bit the roaring twenties flapper – a new breed of modern woman who had ditched the demure, corseted, Victorian idea of what it was to be female. Bobby could dance, could vote and became skilled in applying heavy layers of make-up, previously the preserve of 'loose' women. She cut her long tresses into an artful bob, shed layers of clothing and dressed in outfits that accentuated her feminine sexuality.

As Bobby stepped from the stage of one capital city to another in her sparkling, à la mode dresses, she collected the flyers that announced her troupe's appearances. When newspaper reviewers singled her out, as they often did, she made sure she kept copies of their gushing excitement, every single time.

The Globe Trotters offered a rich evening of entertainment that boasted everything from saucy burlesque to quick-fire comedy routines. Bobby Broadhurst thrilled crowds across the East with 'wonderful

PHOTO BY MING YUEN HONGKONG

The Cranes demonstrates classic chinoiserie inspired by the English colonial aesthetic of the late 1800s. There are only two cranes per 910-millimetre repeat, which makes it both peculiar and effective.

MISS BOBBY BROADHURST

Miss Broadhurst added zest to Carlton's Xmas programme. She is the possessor of a rich soprano voice, and holds all the characteristics of a smart musical comedy artist.
[Photo by Suncott Studio.

14

*Bobby Broadhurst pictured in one of her many onstage costumes. The photograph appeared in the **Shanghai Sunday Times** in the mid-1920s.*

renditions' of 'charming ballads ... her arresting style and rich expressive voice being particularly captivating'. The *Bangkok Daily Mail* noted that her 'very charming contralto voice', used to great effect in songs such as *The Enchantress* and *My Dear Soul*, 'was encored every time'.

The onstage rapture continued throughout the theatres of Singapore, Kuala Lumpur, Penang, Bangkok, Calcutta, Delhi and Karachi before the Globe Trotters turned east for performances in Hong Kong, Shanghai, Tientsin and Peking. Their last performance was in the Yamato Hotel lounge in Dairen, Manchuria, where the tour finally ended in March 1924.

On the sweaty stages of the colonialised east, the Globe Trotters were a hit. Offstage, Bobby and her raffish chums dived into the monied, expatriate social whirl enjoyed by the elite. They explored their surroundings and took pictures of each other. Bobby's photographic collection includes images of exotic camel rides, busy markets and tourist icons such as the Taj Mahal, as well as more intimate scenes at horseracing meets peopled by men who would not look out of place in *The Great Gatsby*.

Bobby forged one particularly significant relationship, with the well-dressed Globe Trotter pianist Wallingford Tate. She kept a series of photographs that portray the two of them together, in which he squires her in the back of smart cars to the front of smart places. Together they explored their new terrain.

One adventure that Broadhurst kept no records of is the romance described in *Queen of the Silk Screens*, the first attempted biography of Broadhurst's life. The author is the late Sherdené Rose, a self-proclaimed psychic who believed Broadhurst communicated with her from beyond the grave but who also conducted interviews with Broadhurst's family and collected some of Broadhurst's letters. The result is a highly melodramatic tale in which Broadhurst, during the Indian leg of the Globe Trotters' tour, romanced royalty in the form of a blue-eyed, Anglo-Indian maharaja from Delhi called Amer Kashif.

Kashif loved Broadhurst desperately, even shooting a tiger in her honour, but Broadhurst chose career over romance, continuing on to China with her troupe and leaving her maharaja behind.

Direct evidence for this delightful fancy has yet to emerge and if Broadhurst made it up to entertain her family, it never will. However, the imagery that surrounds the tale can be seen in Florence Broadhurst's creative output decades later, when she reinvented herself as a designer.

One arresting black and white photograph shows her gazing coquettishly up at a camera, fully made up in heavy lipstick and with dark lines of kohl under her eyes. Her hair is trimmed short in the fashionable Eton cut, a slicked-down shingle. She is wrapped in a dark silk dressing-gown embroidered with flying birds, which would reappear over forty years later in her elegant, landmark image *The Cranes*. She poses by lying on a tiger skin which, once seen, is difficult to separate from the emphatic *Tiger Stripe* pattern that pops up in her eccentric animal print series of designs. Behind her, hanging on a wall, is a rug woven into an intricate tapestry, the likes of which Florence Broadhurst the designer would release onto the market in a range that drew directly upon the best creations of the British Empire.

In this photograph and in this world, Bobby Broadhurst is a butterfly: energetic, beautiful and fantastically decorative. She is surrounded by a kaleidoscope of styles from cultures driven together by colonialism. As Bobby sang and shopped, the political lifestyle that supported her was teetering on the edge of extinction but the warning signs were oblique. What everybody knew, and what Bobby would have heard repeatedly as she and the rest of the Globe Trotters slipped in and out of the cabarets, bars and tea houses of China, was that the real money was in Shanghai.

Following the Globe Trotters' final appearance in Manchuria, Bobby decided to test the waters. She and some of her colleagues would head back to Shanghai and try their luck there, in the commercial centre of colonial Asia. This was a big call. Shanghai contained a wealthy expat

15

*The theatrical Florence pictured
offstage in Bobby Broadhurst
mode, as a heavily made-up
mid-1920s vamp, reclines on
a tiger skin in India.*

community as starved as every other for the diversions of the West but it was also a port where opium and under-age sex were easy to buy. The city was divided: in certain sections the expats had such power that they could not even be prosecuted for crimes under Chinese law; elsewhere the city was so dangerous that they could not walk safely at night.

Bobby, Wallingford Tate, Dick Crichton and a new female performer, Lucina Broadhurst (so-called probably to give the illusion that Bobby had a sister), played a short season at one of the city's hottest venues, The Carlton. The shows turned into an audition, and Bobby then accepted a job with the venue's resident entertainers, the Carlton Sparklers. The outfits worn by these female performers were smaller, tighter and more provocative than anything the young Australian had worn before. In later years, The Carlton would become associated with more sordid entertainment such as bare-knuckle brawls; but what Bobby Broadhurst saw was the glitterati at play, and an idea brewed.

Tiger Stripe – *a forcefully graphic image from Broadhurst's animal print series.*

COURTESY SIGNATURE PRINTS

17

Wallingford Tate had joined another touring theatre group and was clearly hoping Bobby would catch up with him. 'DEAREST', he wrote in a cable dated 15 December 1925, 'FRIGHTFULLY WORRIED. CABLE CONDITION IMMEDIATELY. ALSO SOONEST YOU CAN COME JOIN MUSICAL COMEDY. LOVE WALLY EXCELSIOR BOMBAY.'

It was not to be, and Broadhurst's decision had an added poignancy in that Tate died young, following a bout of typhoid in India several years later. Of all the friends and colleagues Bobby Broadhurst had from this era, Tate's death notice is the only one that she ever kept.

Two weeks after Broadhurst turned Tate down, a local newspaper announced that Bobby Broadhurst had severed her connection with the Carlton Sparklers and that, at the end of the month, she would 'proceed to America to organise her own company for an Australian tour'. Another newspaper reported a slightly different story: 'Bobby … will join at an early date an English comedy company to tour the United States.'

Florence's Globe Trotter colleague, pianist Wallingford Tate, held a very special place in her heart. She kept the cable he sent urging her to join him in 1925 [right] with the word 'DEAREST' crossed out.

Florence launched her first business, the Broadhurst Academy, in Shanghai, on 15 February 1926. She offered expert tuition in everything from dancing and elocution to short-story writing and used every medium available to maximise publicity. She is pictured dancing the Charleston with one of her employees [opposite].

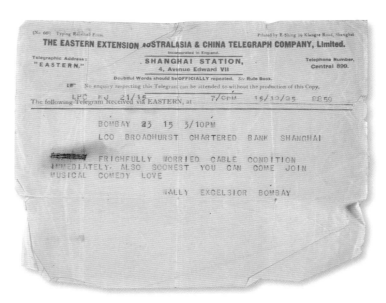

Bobby did neither. She lay low instead. Illness or injury are two possibilities; an unexpected pregnancy a third. Or perhaps she simply needed some time alone to hatch another plan. The cashed-up expats loved to dance, she reasoned. Crazes such as the Charleston swept through London, Paris and New York, and when they did, the rich and bored of faraway Shanghai wanted to join in. Who better than Florence Broadhurst to teach them?

In February 1926, the woman from rural Queensland launched the Broadhurst Academy Incorporated School of the Arts; a finishing school in Shanghai. Here, the 26-year-old would teach the daughters of rich British and American expatriates the sophisticated ins and outs of social life. She found second-floor rooms in a centrally located building on the corner of Nanking and Kiangse roads, pinned some letters after her name and gathered together a group of teachers capable of covering everything from voice lessons to deportment, weight loss and journalism.

She took out newspaper advertisements to announce the Broadhurst Academy's grand opening. *The China Press* ran a picture of her, looking

19

20

Romanesque. These sinuous forms are actually more arabesque than romanesque.

ORGANIZES SUCCESSFUL CONCERT.—Miss B. Broadhurst, A.T.C.L., who was responsible for the highly successful concert given at the B.W.A. headquarters Friday week. Assisting artists were Messrs. Kitain Bros., Ralph Lynn, Higgerman and Walford, and the Misses Peggy James and Bell Leichner.—*Photo by Porter Studio.*

*'Miss B. Broadhurst' appeared in the **Shanghai Sunday Times** on 27 February 1927, after organising a concert at the headquarters of the British Women's Association in Shanghai. The 27-year-old produced a series of soirees for British troops, using every opportunity to liaise with potential new clients of the Broadhurst Academy.*

cheekily chic with a little banjolele. Word had spread that the British Royals were very taken with these instruments, and the caption read: *BANJOLELE WIELDER – Miss Bobby Broadhurst, whose banjolele solo was keenly appreciated when heard over the radio last week. The banjolele has been made famous by the Prince of Wales and other members of royalty. Miss Broadhurst guarantees to teach the banjolele in six lessons in her academy. 38 Kiangse Road.*

Florence used every trick in the book to maximise publicity, even pouncing upon the *North-China Daily News*'s 'Letters to the Editor' page to lock horns with another irate writer over the pressing issue of which was better – the Tango or the Charleston.

'To dance the Charleston is an art,' opined Florence, with the unwavering certainty that would become a trademark during her design era. 'When the royalty of England and the leading society of America give their patronage to a dance, be it Charleston, Blues or camel walk ... those who care will find the correct solution and join in the craze of the world.'

When a new staff member joined, Broadhurst made sure that their picture appeared in the city's newspapers. She started a love affair with social columnists that would continue wherever she was for the rest of her life. She used radio appearances, ran ads in Chinese – Broadhurst was by no means above tapping into the well-to-do locals – and joined the British Women's Association (she was eligible because Australia was part of the British Empire), where she pushed her business further still.

But colonial Shanghai was crumbling. On 12 February 1927, British troops arrived, sparking a general strike. The twelfth of April brought the Shanghai Massacre in which the Guomindang army, led by the embattled President of the Chinese Republic and assisted by Triad gangsters, rounded up and killed communists. Foreigner hatred was growing, as was the communist party, despite brutal efforts to keep it muzzled. A civil war was on the way.

On 25 May 1927, Broadhurst defiantly celebrated Empire Day with a special appearance at the Lyceum Theatre. She sang and performed a banjo solo in what a critic described as 'a thoroughly rousing evening at which *God Save the King* sung by all was the final thrill'.

The sentiments were forthright, but Broadhurst was well aware that it was now too hot to foxtrot in Shanghai. She shed Bobby, packing up her blue Broadhurst Academy-headed writing paper, folding away her press clippings and booking a ticket on a boat headed back home to Australia. The moment she arrived in Bundaberg, en route to her family home in Queensland, she gave a local journalist an interview.

What appeared in the papers a few days later was a profile of Florence Broadhurst the returning heroine entitled 'Five Years Abroad, Experiences in the East, Through the Nanking Revolt'. She described incidents she said she had witnessed, including brutal riots in Nanking. She outlined the sterling performance of the British warship *Emerald*, explained in detail how the Chinese 'can't shoot for nuts', and gave her analysis of exactly what the Japanese needed to do to shore up their position. Then she went home to Mount Perry.

Her father Bill, who now owned the two-storey Mount Perry Hotel, was so proud of his daughter that he talked her into a solo performance in Mount Perry's Federal Hall. Broadhurst quickly made it clear that she would not be staying long, so the performance became a farewell recital which at least one awed local, Mary Shield (who was ten at the time), remembers as if it were yesterday.

Broadhurst walked on stage in a sleeveless, flapper-style, plunging V-necked cream dress that set off her dark bobbed hair and large, soulful eyes beautifully. It hung straight down her upright frame stopping just below the knee, and appeared to be embroidered in some kind of reflective beading off which the stage lights sparkled and radiated incandescently all around the room. She sang a medley of songs in a clear, powerful contralto voice, then made her way into the audience to talk to the local people. 'We were,' says Mary Shield, 'so proud of our Mount Perry girl.'

Several nights after the performance, Broadhurst went out drinking with two local friends, probably at her father's hotel where many of the drinks would have been free. She decided to treat her pals to a spin in her father's expensive new Studebaker car but she took a corner much too fast. She rolled the car, leaving an oil stain in the dirt road, which soaked in so far that it took months to disappear, and took a severe and very serious blow to the head resulting in multiple skull fractures.

Broadhurst spent the following weeks in hospital, recovering from this accident that had almost killed her. 'She had all her hair cut off and her head swathed in bandages,' recalls Mary Shield, who says that the crash put a full stop to Broadhurst's career as a performer. Broadhurst would develop a habit of absent-mindedly stroking what she came to call the 'thin' part of her skull, and later she wrote to her sister Cilla to say that she had had fragments of bone removed. The accident forced Broadhurst to rethink her plans. She had no intention of staying in Mount Perry, or even in Australia, so on Wednesday 19 October 1927 she left Brisbane for London. The voyage marks a cut-off point in the life of Florence Broadhurst. She was about to become a new person entirely.

chapter two

Role play

Who was Madame Pellier? Clearly, a couturier of some note; a discerning individual who understood the needs of women of refinement. She was someone in whose capable hands one could place oneself with utter confidence. After all, *Town and Country News*, a publication doted upon by well-bred, well-dressed British women, said as much in no uncertain terms. On 8 December 1933, the publication ran a full page editorial on the matter, introducing both Madame Pellier and her dress salon 'which is different – and better'.

The interior of this salon is tasteful, discrete and private with partitioned changing rooms, comfortable chairs, and plenty of room to walk about in one's new creation. At first glance, it seems well-appointed: the address is 65 New Bond Street, an eccentric road where the numbers go down one way and up the other, which is reassuringly located in the financial and social heart of London.

This establishment's key calling card is Madame Pellier herself. She appears every inch the well-groomed, artfully made-up fashion advisor.

The Cranes [opposite] is technically difficult to print – its screens are impossible to align and leave gaps between the outlines and the infill; inaccuracies which add to the design's charm.

COURTESY SIGNATURE PRINTS

Her dark, closely cropped hair lies smooth against her head, sweeping back from her face to expose a confident, untroubled brow. Her gaze is relaxed; she displays the kind of casual confidence usually associated with Hollywood actresses. A faint smile plays upon her elegant lips. All in all, she looks remarkably like Florence Broadhurst.

Look a little closer and it becomes clear that Madame Pellier's is not quite what it seems. 'We know there is a need for economy,' *Town and Country*'s editorial runs. 'We know that we cannot spend too freely. We know, too, that it never pays to be other than well-dressed. But how shall one be well-dressed at a lower outlay?'

In 1933 Florence Broadhurst set up shop as Madame Pellier at 65 New Bond Street, London, W1 [opposite left]. Her work got her noticed at the highest level: one of her designs [opposite right] appeared in **Vogue** *on 27 November 1935.*

28

This is where Broadhurst stepped in, at an address that sounded impressive but was actually a revolving door as far as businesses go. Her plan was straightforward: fashionable clothes at affordable cost. 'Prices are amazingly low ... [but] the style really superb,' the article gushes. The woman who comes here wants to look every inch a society success without having to pay the price. Madame Pellier will sort them out.

But just why did Broadhurst become the Bond Street Madame? Her journey began on 19 October 1927, when 'Miss B. Broadhurst', as she called herself in the passenger list, boarded the ocean liner *RMS Orvieto*, a 12 133 tonne Orient Line mail steamer, in Brisbane. The ship sailed to Sydney and picked up more passengers, before visiting Melbourne, Adelaide and Fremantle. It then moved into international waters on a six-week voyage that would take in Colombo, Suez, Port Said, Naples, Toulon and Gibraltar. Miss B. Broadhurst left the boat at its final destination – London.

The 28-year-old hit the ground running. By 9 February 1928, she was enjoying the royal box at Wembley Stadium and the Greyhound Racecourse. In June, she told a friend she had backed 'nearly all the horses in the derby' and by August she was treating herself to a summer holiday in Paris.

PARIS via PELLIER

Paris, being Paris, is sometimes a little over-confident . . . flinging into the picture new modes that neither the English mind can cherish nor the English figure wear.

A Frenchwoman can sometimes go to extremes in style and pattern that would make her English cousin look "fancy dress." This season, France, as you know, is going everything from Abyssinian to Bersaglier . . . with military millinery Renaissance gownery . . . classical negligee.

And "shirring" and "draping" are becoming the most overworked words in the couturiers' vocabulary.

All very whimsical and smart in moderation. IN MODERATION. Which is precisely where Madame Pellier sweeps in. The new Pellier models are founded on Paris but interpreted into smartest possible English. All that the Pellier models have lost is a danger of looking ridiculous. And ah, how much they have gained! Whatever the hour or the occasion, you could never be safer than in a Pellier creation!

Pellier Ltd

(MADAME PELLIER)

**65 NEW BOND STREET
LONDON, W.I**

the Fortnight

Colourful plaid clothes this navy wool coat. 8 guineas. Pellier, Bond Street

A becoming perch, a feather brush . . Terret black felt military hat. 2½ guineas

Dorville's coral wool afternoon dress. Softly gathered. 8½ guineas. Forgeron, South Molton Street

Cocktail dress angel sleeves. ruffle gold belt. 13 guineas. Dorville model from Fenwick

Low heeled sandal, 16s 9d.; gold on silver kid; 29s 6d.; crêpe high instep in brocade, 29s 6d. Abbott, Oxford Street

Broadhurst made a beeline for Paris's playgrounds of the rich and
flirtatious – venues such as the Casino de la Foret and Touquet Tennis
Club where bright young bankers, lawyers and stockbrokers were likely
to be found amusing themselves. She met and quickly became engaged
to such a person – a 34-year-old stockbroker named Percy Walter
Gladstone Kann.

As suitors go, the dashing Percy Kann was a world away from any
of the men Broadhurst had involved herself with before. His elderly
father, eighty-year-old John Baptiste Joseph Kann, was also a stockbroker:
a partner in the stock and share broking firm A.G. Schiff & Co. in
Warnford Court, a prestigious address opposite the London Stock
Exchange, itself in the heart of the city.

John Kann, like Louisa, his seventy-year-old wife, was Austrian by
birth and British by naturalisation. The couple relocated to England
before the arrival in 1884 of their eldest daughter Annie, who was born
in the London suburb of Stoke Newington. They had a child every two
years after Annie's birth: John in 1886, Winifred in 1888 and Grace
in 1890.

Percy appeared on the scene five years later, in 1885. His birthplace
is listed as Hampstead. By the time the youngster was three, his father
joined the stock exchange and his financial acumen quickly began
paying dividends. In the 1920s the Kanns moved further upmarket,
to Lyne Hill House, an impressive, sprawling property outside the
River Thames town of Chertsey in Surrey.

World War I had just ended and Percy, like most other young British
men, had done his bit. On 18 February 1925, the returned soldier
decided to follow in his father's footsteps. In his applicant's statement
to join the stock exchange, he explained, in brief, his history.

'In September 1916, at the age of 21, I was serving as 2nd Lieutenant
in the 1st Bn. The Buffs in France. In 19-- [date obscured by tightly
sewn binding] I transferred to the Tank Corps from which I was
gazetted out as a Captain in April 1919.'

*Images such as **Tudor Floral**
[opposite] appeared in rich
upholstery fabrics of the
1800s but are very rarely
manipulated into this scale.*

31

COURTESY SIGNATURE PRINTS

'In Jan. 1920 I joined Messrs A.G. Schiff & Co. as a Clerk, & in March 1921 entered -? [word obscured] House as Unauthorised Clerk.'

Percy, then thirty and living with his parents at Lyne Hill House, proposed to act as a broker's clerk. He was admitted in March 1925. His was a family that did things properly, so when Broadhurst agreed to marry Percy, the Kanns made sure social niceties were attended to. In the time-honoured tradition, on Friday 7 June 1929, *The Times* announced the forthcoming nuptial of Percy Kann and Florence Broadhurst.

Florence Broadhurst married Percy Kann on Friday 7 June 1929 at London's Brompton Oratory. She kept this photograph, taken by the prestigious London studio Vandyk of Buckingham Palace Road, and on the day, kept her real age to herself.

32

Their wedding took place on Saturday 22 June 1929. The venue was impressive – the Roman Catholic Church at the Brompton Oratory, an imposing, white stone, Byzantine building beside the Victoria and Albert Museum in Kensington. Father A. Hawarden presided over the ceremony. On her wedding certificate Broadhurst declared her age as twenty-seven rather than twenty-nine.

The wedding photographer was the best that money could buy: the prestigious Vandyk Studio, of 41 Buckingham Palace Road, whose stationery proudly trumpeted that the business operated 'By Appointment to King George V' and who could claim as its clients a roll call of European royals. No expense was spared and before the wedding, as the letters cited in the docudrama *Unfolding Florence* show, John Kann asked Florence's parents for 'perhaps £2000' towards expenses. The request would make her sister Cilla distrust Florence's motives from then on.

Despite the pomp and ceremony of Broadhurst's big day, the only memento she kept of the unique occasion was a photograph taken by Vandyk as a blushing bride. She is beautifully demure in a flowing cream wedding gown with diaphanous veil and carrying a large bouquet of flowers. There is no record of the guests or reception and no list of presents, notes from guests or telegrams from family members unable to attend. There is emphatically no picture of her husband.

The Kanns moved in to 26 Queen's Road, St John's Wood, NW8, but they had a shock coming. In October 1929, Wall Street crashed, precipitating a stock market dive that shuddered across Europe's financial capitals and ushered in the Great Depression.

Within two years the career of Percy's elderly father was over. What should be his 1931 entry in the official list of stock exchange members is crossed through in ink and his firm A.G. Schiff & Co. is wiped from the records. That there is no record of the Kanns living at their country mansion Lyne Hill House beyond 1932, when stocks and shares hit rock bottom, suggests that the family may have been caught up in the financial disaster. Percy Kann appears in the 1932/3 list of stock exchange members, where his business address is given as 3/4 Great Winchester Street, London. The following year he, too, disappears from the list.

But the indefatigable Broadhurst had another string to her bow. Before her marriage she earned money working for upper-crust fashion houses, including Madame Corot Ltd, a well-established business at 33 Old Bond St, W1, and W.W. Reville-Terry of Grosvenor Square, which clad minor royals such as the stylish Queen Maud of Norway. She had spent her time at these establishments wisely.

The key to their success, Broadhurst realised, lay beyond the dressmaking skills which she had learnt as a child in rural Queensland. They created fashions, yes, but at heart these outfits were all about networking, and the companies that endured had at their head somebody who would attract potential clients.

Marriage had given Florence a new surname but she wanted to become somebody else again. She developed a plan to create her own Bond Street fashion house by stepping into the role of a French couturier. After all, she later explained, the head of such an outfit just had to have a French name.

In 1933 Madame Pellier was born. She was French, beautiful and painfully chic; a thorough, exacting woman who understood couture

Fanciful and twisted, **Centrepoint Medallion** *[opposite] is heraldic in layout, drawn with a whimsical softness.*

35

The Pellier calling card was an essential tool, an assurance that this fashionable dress designer meant business.

and the rigours required to attain it. Women's fashions had moved on from the boyish exuberance of the twenties. The sexy silhouette was back and being created in new fabrics such as rayon. Madame Pellier understood. She was all woman, the image of her time and the perfect figurehead for a fashion house which had, on paper at least, two directors behind it: Florence Broadhurst and her husband Percy Kann.

The first thing Madame Pellier needed was a salon in which to entertain her clients. The premises at 65 New Bond Street, on the corner of Brook Street in the bustling centre of London, were perfect – discreet, convenient and quiet. Madame Pellier had the place dressed up with comfortable chairs in which relatives or friends squiring her clients could sit and wait; there were mannequins upon which she would place flowing Pellier gowns, and plenty of flowers arranged in vases. She called the tasteful interior Pellier's 'Grey Salon', and as soon as it was ready she let her public know she was ready to receive them.

She took out advertisements in magazines that introduced Pellier as 'a genuine dress artist ... one of the most original dress designers'. At first she aimed her sights relatively modestly but this would soon change. The first entry Pellier's establishment takes in the 1934 London Post Office Director lists her business as 'Pellier Ltd – gowns'. Within twelve months, Madame Pellier had bolder claims to make. In 1935, 1936 and 1937 the entry reads 'Pellier Ltd – court dressmakers'.

Madame Pellier's clients included performers and socialites. One particularly notable customer, the raven-haired concert pianist named Harriet Cohen, was so grateful that she sent Madame Pellier a black and white photograph of herself dressed in a stunning lace creation that Pellier had presumably created for her. The inscription reads, 'Pellier. With thanks from Harriet Cohen.'

Two other performers, a man and a woman who signed their names as simply Jillette and Oliver, sent the couturier a rather racy black and white studio shot of their heads and naked shoulders. They wrote on it: 'To Madame Pellier/The Inspiration of the "Little Blue Shop"/ from Jillette & Oliver 1934.'

Madame Pellier kept other images that related to her achievements, including photographs of two sisters, Helene and Rose Abouchanab. These fresh-faced young women are wealthy debutantes whose family wanted a permanent record of their entry into society. Helene and Rose are photographed individually in a studio dressed in formal evening gowns while standing on a Hellenic pedestal. They wear long, light-coloured, figure-hugging robes – presumably Pellier creations – with trains that coil around their feet. Three-quarter length evening gloves, expensive jewellery, dark bobbed hair, heavy make-up and even some retouching complete the picture.

Had Pellier descended into the Bond Street whirl ten years earlier, and had she not become embroiled in legal action with Madame Corot over whether she had stolen its client list, she might have left more of a footprint among the upper classes she longed to work with. But the roaring twenties were over, as was the penchant for frivolous recklessness. Times were tough and most fashionable clothes – with the exception of furs and hats – were now considered luxuries that fewer and fewer women could afford. This was a challenging time for Madame Pellier, both in her business and in her marriage.

In 1935, Leonard Lloyd Lewis, a fruit merchant, met Madame Pellier at her Bond Street dress salon. '[She was] doing a roaring trade among the upper crust,' he proudly told the *Australian Women's Weekly* shortly after her death. The article was published on 16 November 1977, and Lewis outlined Broadhurst's until-then-secret past completely. He also added a few new fantasies into the mix: her family, Lewis claimed, were 'sugar people'; Dame Clara Butt had introduced her as a singing star when she was sixteen; Broadhurst wrote prolific articles for Australian newspapers while living in China, and when Lewis left her for another woman, Broadhurst was very friendly to Lewis's new love.

38

Wallpaper was developed centuries ago as a cheap substitute for tapestry. Broadhurst's **Florentine Tapestry** *is a later – and larger – take on motifs used in the early Renaissance. It now graces nightclub walls in Sydney.*

HANDPRINTED BY FLORENCE BROADHURST WALLPAPERS SYDNEY

FLORENTINE "P.26

SYDNEY, AUSTRALIA # TRIM WITH STRAIGHTEDGE

*Broadhurst was known for designs such as **Hessian**, which give otherwise plain base papers the illusion of having a texture woven through them.*

40

His account of their first meeting does not cast him in a particularly noble light, which gives it a perverse ring of truth. 'It was a storybook meeting. I was a good-looking twenty-three and Florence was a glamorous thirty-six. It was like a young man meeting a film star. I was instantly enamoured. From that moment I didn't leave her side for twenty-six years.'

Certainly by 11 February 1936, Broadhurst was peeling herself away from her married name. She bought a dyed ermine coat for £122, gave her address as c/o Pellier, 65 New Bond St and used the name Miss Broadhurst. Leonard Lewis took full credit for the break-up of the Kann marriage. 'Soon after we met she and Percy were divorced,' he said. 'We were married in London before the war.'

Lewis lived this lie, and the subsequent lie of having divorced Florence in 1961, until just before his death in 1989. When I asked Robert Lloyd-Lewis for details of his parents' marriage and divorce in order to obtain the relevant certificates, he replied bluntly, 'you won't find them' before going on to explain that they never actually married.

Robert Lloyd-Lewis had no idea this was the case until his terminally ill father finally revealed that fact during their last holiday together. His mother never discussed it, and the reason for their decision not to marry remains unclear. When his parents met, society was still struggling with marital break-up, as King Edward VIII's 1936 abdication for the love of divorcee Mrs Wallis Simpson showed only too well.

Broadhurst's situation was trickier still. She had married as a Catholic, and Catholic divorces were not easy to obtain. Even so, she was determined to make a life with Leonard Lewis. It involved jettisoning both of her previous names – Madame Pellier, who disappears from all business records at around this time; and Mrs Florence Kann. She instead became Mrs Lewis, and moved in with her 'husband' to 134 Kensington Park Road, London.

In 1938, at the age of 39, 'Mrs Lewis' became pregnant. She and Lewis wanted their child but problems began before the birth when

Florence was rushed into Hammersmith Hospital in central London with albumen poisoning. She was also coping with bad news from Australia. Her mother Margaret had become extremely ill. The timing was terrible – Florence could not even consider visiting Australia. Her mother died before she could see her.

It was the driest April on record and as May approached, the curious weather continued with an unseasonal cool front. Treacherous fogs hit the capital. Florence, still in hospital, went into labour and on hearing the news Leonard jumped into his car and rushed to be by her side. He crashed his car in the fog, splitting open his pancreas. The family would later joke that their son's birth had resulted in both parents being hospitalised at the same time.

On Wednesday 3 May, Florence gave birth to her only child. Although he is named 'Robin Lloyd Lewis' on the birth certificate that his parents registered four weeks later, and would be called Robin by his Australian grandfather for the rest of his life, his parents dubbed him 'Robert' and the name stuck. They also hyphenated his surname on his first passport. Leonard's injury had an unforeseeable result. When World War II broke out in September of the following year, he would be deemed unfit for active service. As a result, he spent the entire war based at home with his family.

Lloyd-Lewis's earliest recollections of those days are strained through a child's eye view of World War II: nightly blackouts, having his very own gasmask and being hurried into the bombshelter under their roomy two-storey home in Higher Drive, Banstead – a Surrey suburb just south of London. He remembers not understanding his mother's furious cries of 'you have got to move quickly' when the air raid sirens started wailing. He also recalls emerging after an all-clear sounded to find shrapnel stuck in his bedhead just inches away from where he slept, and that Mr Hitler had bombed his tricycle, as well as the rest of the back garden.

41

The Lewis residence backed onto a golf course and young Lloyd-Lewis was fascinated by the anti-aircraft guns he could see rolling up and down the railway line. He knew all about enemy raids and the heroic men who set blimps up in the sky in a desperate attempt to stop the evil Nazis bombing London. Lloyd-Lewis does not remember being scared – 'I just thought that's the way the world is' – but he does remember seeing that his mother clearly was on occasion. He also recalls that his mother and father were up to their necks in the war effort.

Leonard Lewis was posted to the nearby Surrey town of Cheam where he ran a factory making bombsights, the aircraft devices used for aiming bombs. It was a top secret enterprise – the factory was hidden inside a church which always had somebody posted on the roof as a lookout. When the air-raid siren went, the lookout checked which way the bombers were heading and if they were not coming their way, the engineers inside the church just kept on working. Once made, the bombsights were packed into cartons and discreetly delivered. Lloyd-Lewis recalls his father making delivery runs with cartons of bombsights stacked up in the back of his car.

Bacchus Tapestry [opposite], unused since Broadhurst's day, is an original hand-drawn artwork. This image has been digitally coloured.

COURTESY SIGNATURE PRINTS

42

But Lewis's job also took him further afield, to Northern Ireland and to Wales. He invariably returned with moulds of butter and shoulders of pork – gold dust in the grim war days of rationing and coupons. Lloyd-Lewis remembers eating so much that he would make himself sick 'because it was so rich and you weren't used to it. But it was meat. You over-ate, you got indigestion, you were unwell'.

After the war, Lloyd-Lewis studied his mother's travel documents and realised that she, too, had travelled, presumably to obtain mainly fabrics, which she would make into soft furnishings such as curtains, and sell. But Mrs Lewis also had a public role in wartime activities. She became involved in special events in London and kept photographs of the most auspicious occasions. She opened the Lewis home to Australian servicemen on leave. The house had a piano, which the guests used for impromptu singalongs. Robert never heard his mother join in. In fact, he never heard his mother sing at all.

A bottle-blonde Broadhurst as photographed for her passport. The picture is marked 'England 39–45/ During War'.

44

The grim, bleak days of war with Germany turned into weeks, then months, then years. Britain became used to living under the threat of the Third Reich and for her role as part of the resistance Florence changed her appearance yet again. As Mrs Lewis, her clothes were chic, austere and military-influenced in the patriotic, practical, restrained style of the times. She grew her hair so that her moody dark locks became glamorous, feminine tresses. Then she bleached her hair blonde, Hollywood starlet style. The effect was utterly à la mode but so thoroughly Aryan that, had the Germans won the war, says her son, 'she would definitely have got away with it'.

As the conflict drew to a close, the Lewis family moved to 26 Mill Road, Worthing, a West Sussex town on the south coast of England. Five-year-old Robert found himself packed off to boarding school near Brighton so close to their home that he could have been a day boy, something that rankles to this day. 'My mother said that it would be better for me, and deep down I believed that it would be better for my mother,' he says. 'Deep down ... I felt as though I had been rejected and pushed away. That I was excess baggage.'

He was shuttled from one boarding school to another until the post-war reopening of Sompting Abbott Preparatory School, an expensive, history-laden institution. Here, says Lloyd-Lewis, the rationale was that a good dose of the Bible and a good belting would do every child wonders. 'I don't think in later life I've really suffered that much,' he adds.

Leonard Lewis bought an ex-RNL lifeboat, the *Guernsey*. There was a very good reason – a fishing licence meant an extra ration card, and the family could certainly do with that. Mrs Lewis also bought her own boating licence, one that enabled her to operate a slow passenger boat from Brighton's West Pier. Running a charter boat was an interesting idea but Florence, by now an astute businesswoman, did not have time to see the project through to its fruition. She had another, more pressing problem to deal with. Leonard had met somebody else.

Lloyd-Lewis was far too young to understand what was happening but
he has since pieced it together pretty clearly. He remembers his father
leaving him outside a certain woman's house, going in, and telling him
to be good until his father came back outside. His mother was furious.
She wanted none of it, nipping the affair in the bud by forcing a family
move to her homeland of Australia, a country where Leonard would
have to start again. And she made absolutely sure that Leonard left the
country first.

Broadhurst wanted her son to experience the height of British pomp
and ceremony before she whisked him off to the new world; so, on
20 November 1947, she made sure he witnessed a fairytale. In plum-
voiced, breathless tones BBC radio relayed the news to everybody who
could not be there in person:

*'The huge crowd that's on either side of the Mall are now getting their first
glimpse of Princess Elizabeth and her wedding dress. It's of ivory white
satin and the whole dress is most delicately embroidered with seed pearls and
crystals and garlands of white York roses entwined with ears of Corn. It is a
most beautiful dress.'*

Princess Elizabeth – young, slender and beautiful – was marrying
her distant cousin, the dashing Lieutenant Philip Mountbatten. The
wedding was a welcome spectacle in the post-war, wintry gloom and
thousands of excited onlookers lined the Mall to see the dream unfold.
Right at the front of the flag-waving crowd stood Florence Lewis and
her nine-year-old son Robert, who watched in wide-eyed amazement
as the radiant princess passed by, just metres away, in her splendid,
horse-drawn carriage.

Broadhurst would later tell people that it was upon this star-studded
occasion that she first met the Queen Mother. It is an unlikely story
and one which her son, who was with her all day, certainly does
not remember. What he does recall is that she was insistent that he
experience this, and one other massive spectacle – the stunning neon

45

lights of Piccadilly being switched back on after the war. 'You've got to see this, son, before we go,' she told him.

Mother and son left their life in England by stepping aboard the *Orontes 1949* at London's Tilbury Docks. Leonard Lewis had gone on ahead but young Robert barely cared. He loved boats and was about to begin the most incredible voyage he could imagine on the largest ship he had ever seen. To the boy, the *Orontes 1949* was massive: 638.2 feet long, 75.2 feet wide and weighing in at 20 097 tonnes. It had seen active service during the war but there was no sign of that now. It had a top speed of 18 knots, two buff: yellow funnels and room for 1112 third-class passengers and 460 first-class passengers. Mrs Lewis and her son were firmly part of the latter.

The pair shared a large cabin one floor below the main deck but Robert cared little for its creature comforts. All he could see was a highly varnished, floating playground – the height of plushness for passengers underpinned by relentless graft from the crew. There were other children on board but to him they were just kids. What he wanted was the run of the ship; and much to his mother's consternation, he acted as though he had it.

'I used to disappear and you could find me anywhere from the focsle to the engine room – in places where children were probably never supposed to be,' he says. 'I remember coming through the Bay of Biscay. There was a gale and I [was] … standing on the deck just below the bridge, water's flying over the top, spraying everywhere. Oh, it was beautiful. My mother was sending the crew out to find me: "He's swept overboard, my little boy".' Lloyd-Lewis belly-laughs. 'I wanted to follow the crewmen when [they] scrubbed the deck. I wanted to be in the Navy.'

Broadhurst had little interest in cooping her exuberant child up but she did require him to do his duty. 'I was a good little English boy, and the good little English boy wore his sandals and socks and [was] seen

Hollow Squares [opposite], a late-sixties, modern geometric graphic, is one of a series of Broadhurst designs that deliberately plays with dimension.
COURTESY SIGNATURE PRINTS

47

Robert Lloyd-Lewis during the wartime years in the family garden. His tricycle did not survive the war.

Honeycomb [opposite], a Moroccan motif that now decorates nightclubs and restaurants in London, Auckland and Dubai.

COURTESY SIGNATURE PRINTS

and not heard. [I] had no opinion,' he recalls. His mother's place was elsewhere – on the captain's table for dinner, beautifully made up and smartly dressed.

For Lloyd-Lewis, this was a moment of awakening. He had never spent this much time with his mother before. 'I realised then that you had to fit around what was obviously important to her. Being seen in the right place at the right time ... Even at that early age you woke up to the fact that this is what Mum does.'

The days rolled by in a blur of ocean spray, sun, rain, wind and swell. Suddenly, the little English boy's tenth birthday was upon him. He celebrated it in the Australian waters between Fremantle and Melbourne. Every now again Robert found himself quizzing his mother. Where did she come from? What did she do before the war?

'Oh darling, that's so long ago, I can't even remember,' she would reply before segueing into a monologue that would become, for Robert, a mantra. What his mother wanted to talk about – apart from exactly what Leonard had done that was making them take this trip – was her dread of becoming elderly and dependent. 'I don't want to sit in a hospital bed with somebody having to change me because I've wet myself,' she told her son. He remembers hearing it 'almost continually. It was one of her greatest fears [...] that she would one day be old and incapacitated.'

The Florence Broadhurst who stepped off that steamer in Australia was far from either. To her son, she was as energetic, forceful and decisive as ever. Before he could even say 'crumbs', in an accent that was as thoroughly English as his mother's had become, he and his family were settled in a flat in the beachside Sydney suburb of Manly.

While his parents organised their digs into some sort of order, Robert only had eyes for Manly's long, white arc of sand and for the treats of child-hood. His aunt Cilla appeared and took the youngster to a Greek cafe

on the Manly Corso. 'She bought me my first milkshake,' he recalls. 'I'd come from a country where ... milk was not plentiful, so I remember it. A whole milkshake.'

For young Robert the shocks kept coming. His father bought a green Studebaker utility and drove the family north to meet his mother's relatives in Mount Perry. 'Those roads were all dirt,' says Lloyd-Lewis who had never seen anything like the endless tracts of landscape and bizarre creatures bouncing about outside the car.

'It was such a vast country. I had no idea. I had come from the south of London to the coastline of Worthing [and] I thought that was a big drive. This took days.'

The family journeyed beyond Brisbane, inland through bushland and rough rolling fields that never seemed to end. Finally, they arrived at Mount Perry, a quiet rural outpost with wide, dusty roads, beautifully constructed weatherboard houses and, as far as Broadhurst's thoroughly unacclimatised son could see, very little else at all.

A fun fashion favourite, Aubrey [opposite] is a particular hit in swimwear.
COURTESY SIGNATURE PRINTS

51

Broadhurst's father Bill and her older sister May lived in a house on the outskirts of town called 'The Pines'. It was an elegant, free-standing, gracious building with a well-tended garden. Even so, young Lloyd-Lewis was gobsmacked.

'I couldn't understand [it],' he says. 'My mother – this woman who I knew was gentry – this is where she came from?' Questioned as to how he knew she was gentry, Lloyd-Lewis pauses. 'She acted the part, and was able to command respect without question, [that] of somebody who was accustomed to it, by background,' he replies. 'If she walked into a hotel, she would get the best suite, even if it meant moving people.' Here, Florence Broadhurst was just one of the girls – a long-lost sister returning home.

But right from the start there was trouble. Both of Florence's sisters, May and Cilla, suspected she had ulterior motives in coming back

*Fruit Vine's larger-than-life
motif echoes designs found on
Grecian vases.*

to Australia. May had never married, nor had she ever moved out of
the family home. When their mother died in 1938 it was she who
looked after their father and she who helped out with the stock.
Lloyd-Lewis recalls tensions bubbling up between the sisters almost
immediately, seemingly fuelled by Bill's delight in seeing Florence
once more.

'She was assumed to be the favoured one, the prodigal son. Perhaps they
thought she was coming to take something that belonged to them. I
know that May was very upset she had come back. [I] got the feeling
that May saw me as an intruder in the relationship between father and
daughter. Because I was there, he [Bill] would say [to me] things like:
"Come on, we've got to go and dig water holes in the creek".'

Young Lloyd-Lewis had a ball with his grandfather, learning skills that
he had only ever dreamed of in the tame, manicured heart of southern
England. Here, he could ride, herd and camp, boil billy tea over a fire
in the middle of the bush with a man who was getting on in years but
whose energy and work ethic were second only to his mother's.

'If you want to ride this pony you can, no problem,' Bill told his
grandson. 'But you have to feed it, muck out its stable, look after it.'

Back in Manly, Florence's family began their new life in earnest.
Leonard took over a motor dealership in Penrith 50 kilometres west
of Sydney but decided fairly quickly it was too far and started running
a Shell service station that sold cars as well as petrol on nearby Spit
Road. Robert had a short spell at a Christian Brothers' school in Manly
before being sent to yet another boarding school: Barker College, an
imposing 1890-built Anglican school in the northern Sydney suburb
of Hornsby. Again, it was so close that he could have been a day boy.

His mother dived into painting, and became friends with a local artist.
She began to hatch a new plan. She would become a noted painter.
All she had to do was pick a subject, and what better than the Australian
landscape so unfamiliar to her 'husband' and son?

She organised a three-month trip through the bush to paint enough canvasses for her first exhibition, and decided to base herself at her father's home in Mount Perry.

By this time, May had died and Cilla had moved in to look after their ageing father. She was so distrustful of Florence that she would not even let her into the family home. Local stockman Ted Bettiens observed Leonard, Robert, Florence and her artist friend having to camp in a nearby gully. 'They used to go to a hotel for showers and that,' he laughs. 'There was a feud between the two sisters. I was caught in the middle, this one asked me what that one said, and then the other one did the same ... I suppose [Cilla] thought Florence was coming to get something she might get.'

In fact, Broadhurst's visit was entirely above board. She and her artist friend roamed around Bill's property getting Ted Bettiens to cut into the bark of trees and extract different-coloured saps that they could use as pigments. Lewis, who did not appear to Bettiens to be the least bit interested in the arty pair's work, drove them about. This was the first time Bettiens had met Broadhurst. A lot of people in Mount Perry 'reckoned she was a snob because she had an educated voice', he recalls. He liked her. 'I just thought she was educated.'

During Broadhurst's wallpaper era, she would produce a number of designs which harked back to the bush. One of the most obvious, *Aboriginal Rock Art*, is amusing in its naivety – a Hanna-Barbera interpretation of cave paintings that show straight-legged, pear-shaped kangaroos bounding through a little crowd of stick figures with spears. It is not Broadhurst's best work.

By 1954, Florence Broadhurst was back in Sydney, and ready to launch her new career. Both the *Sydney Morning Herald* and the *Daily Telegraph* happily covered her exploits and both articles appeared, appropriately enough, on Thursday 1 April.

Florence Broadhurst photographed at work on a night-time scene at Sydney's Trocadero.

53

Under the headline 'She Came To Rest – And Stayed To Paint,' the *SMH* told the story of 'Mrs L. Broadhurst [sic], an Englishwoman who in 3½ years has painted 200 Australian landscapes – snowfields and desert, the bush and the Barrier Reef.' Mr and Mrs Broadhurst [sic] and their son had come to Australia for a holiday – 'and none of them wanted to go back', apparently. Mrs Broadhurst told the newspaper she would exhibit her paintings 'in America and England next year'. She had 'spent 10 years studying in Paris' where she went to train as a singer before earning money designing clothes. The war had put paid to everything but when she arrived in this fresh new land, she simply couldn't resist the idea of immortalising it on canvas.

The Egrets [opposite] display unusual character and stature. Each of the standing birds is 40 centimetres tall.

54

COURTESY SIGNATURE PRINTS

The Daily Telegraph relayed how 'a dynamic fair-haired English artist now in Sydney has given herself 12 months "to paint the story of Australia" to show the world.' The article, about Broadhurst's forthcoming exhibition at the city's David Jones store, painted a picture of a woman who had motored 10 000 miles through 'Queensland, Central Australia and New South Wales'. Broadhurst said she would go abroad with her 'picture story' early the following year. 'She will start with exhibitions in New York, Canada, London and Paris,' the story trilled. 'Sir Winston Churchill was thrilled with a painting of Alice Springs which Florence sent him for Christmas at his own request.'

Broadhurst told the press she worked at her painting seven days a week, had studied dress designing and was a pianist, a professional singer and a public speaker. She was also, chipped in Leonard Lewis, 'a really good cook'.

On 18 May 1954, a larger article appeared, coinciding with the exhibition opening. Here, Broadhurst, really went to town. Leonard Lloyd-Lewis was hyphenating his name. He became 'a financier'. In future articles he would upgrade further still, reaching the pinnacle of his career, on paper at least, as a 'business tycoon'.

Broadhurst described herself as a 'concert singer in London and Paris [who] gave up singing for painting a few years before she came

to Australia'. She said she was 'a former voluntary speaker for Britain's
Women-for-Westminster movement (which clamoured for more
women members of Parliament)' and a 'voluntary member of the
Conservative Party's panel of speakers'.

She announced that she wanted to become Australia's Ambassadress
and launched a competition to find a national dress. The press lapped
it up. 'We've had to wait for an Englishwoman to sense the need for
a new symbol of waratah and wattle spirit with which Henry Lawson
and his contemporaries stirred our somewhat lethargic embers of
patriotism 50 years ago,' came one opinion-maker's reply.

According to the *Australia Magazine* (18 May 1954), 'Miss Broadhurst
lectures in Australia on art and woman's place in world affairs, and
after lectures usually gives a painting of hers away to be raffled for
charity.' In this report, Winston Churchill gets a painting of the
Macdonnell Ranges rather than Alice Springs, but whatever the
truth (and the Churchill Archives Centre contains no record of the
statesman receiving either painting, nor any mention of Broadhurst
under any of her names) her mission is clear. She wants to give the
English a better idea of what Australia is really like. Mind you, she is
also keen to sell her work. 'Said she ... "some of the best people have
bought them, paying between 60 and 80 guineas".'

One of the major pieces in this exhibition was a dramatic, desolate
picture of the main road of Mount Perry. Shadows lie across the hot,
empty streetscape, so bereft of any form of life it has the haunted air
of a ghost town. The only building identifiable by name is the imposing
Grand Hotel. It is the pub that her father owned and her mother
had run but Broadhurst does not let on to the public that there is any
personal connection between herself and the building. 'There's always
an old hotel, you know,' Broadhurst cheekily told the newspaper.

Up in Queensland, her family was fuming. Bill sounded off to his mate
Les Jensen that his daughter should not be telling people she was came

*The main road of Mount Perry
circa 1910.*

*Arabian Birds [opposite]
coloured from original
artwork, is richly textured
and unusually intricate.*

COURTESY SIGNATURE PRINTS

57

Japanese Floral – an essay in opulent simplicity.

58

from England and that she was 'trying to be something she wasn't'. Cilla was livid, too. Says Robert Lloyd-Lewis of Broadhurst's re-creation of her identity as a woman who had been born and bred in Britain, 'I don't think she was ashamed in any way [of her background]. I think that it suited her purpose not so say that she came from Mount Perry. I knew, obviously her sister knew, and maybe that was part of the tension between [them], that she was receiving publicity and that people's perception was that she was English ... Maybe that's what they were annoyed about: "You are saying that we are not good enough for you. The illusion that you are creating is that you don't have a family."'

Listen to Lloyd-Lewis describe his childhood and you could come away with the impression that Broadhurst may as well not even have had a son. Lloyd-Lewis felt shut out from the family home in Manly forever being sent away on sports camps or over to friends' houses to stay. When he was at home, and in the kind of trouble that teenage boys seem drawn to, he recalls his mother's reaction as being rather egotistical. On one occasion he locked horns with another local lad and ended up being frog-marched home by a police officer who told his mother that if this happened again young Robert would be taken down to the station and charged. Broadhurst was furious. '[Don't] you drag my name through the papers,' she raved at her son. 'If the papers get hold of this ...'. 'It was about the perception of her reputation,' he says. 'All I did was have an altercation with another boy and create a bit of a disturbance.'

Every now and again, people from his mother's previous lives would flicker past. Ralph Sawyer, who had toured with Broadhurst across Asia, brought the international ballet star and actor Sir Robert Helpmann to visit the Broadhursts' Manly home in 1952. It prompted Lloyd-Lewis to ask her again about her life before him. 'Tell me all about it,' he would beg. 'She'd say, "When you're older." But I was never old enough.'

Occasionally, Lloyd-Lewis would spend a weekend away from his
boarding school and at home. He remembers being quite happy to
get back to his dormitory at the end of it. 'There were ... strains in the
relationship between father and mother at that time,' he says carefully.
When he did see his mother, he does not recall hugs and kisses, and
describes her as 'fairly distant'. That said, she did make time for him,
Lloyd-Lewis says, 'so mixed in with the restraint was an awful amount
of pride.'

The first time he played for the combined association schools first
15 rugby team, Broadhurst was there. 'My father was at the races but
she was there,' he recounts. 'I didn't see her, but in a letter that week
she said, "You played a very good game and you were quite sporting
when you pulled back [from someone I could have punched] and then
gave them a lift off the ground." In other words she was telling me,
"I was there. I saw it."' She did not watch him play in the national
schoolboy team – she realised during that first match that the game
was more important than she was, he says. But the fact that she did
show her face at that event, he muses, might have been her way of
saying, 'I want to have a very independent young man as a son. She
certainly did not want me to become my father.' For what Broadhurst
was facing while Robert was away at school was a situation in which
the impulsive Leonard had allowed a passion to become a serious
weakness. The problem was gambling.

Lloyd-Lewis remembers his father coming home from a day at the
races and literally covering the table with money, only to lose it all
the next week. 'I think that made my mother a very secretive person,'
he says. 'I remember her saying to me on one occasion in the school
holidays, "If he offers you any money, take it. Put it in your bank
account." She would always have a shoebox and even when my father
flew over [to Sydney] after her death, he said, "Now don't forget
to look through the house properly, because your mother will have
squirrelled cash, money, all over the place".'

Broadhurst did hide money from Lewis. He started buying horses, something that would later become a benign hobby of hers, but they had a habit of running up vet and training fees and when the big day came they would be lame. Every now and again mother and son would visit the races with Lewis. 'By the third race he would be hundreds of thousands up, and by the last race it would be "Geez, you got money for the bridge toll home?" '

By 1955, things were easing up. Lloyd-Lewis had left school the previous year as a seventeen-year-old, so £100 a term no longer had to be found for fees. His father had struck a deal with the finance company Australian Guarantee Corporation to sell repossessed vehicles and they opened a car and truck yard in Crows Nest. But Broadhurst's scheme of becoming a financially independent artist was floundering.

The *Sydney Morning Herald* was unkind about her first major exhibition and her talent, concluding that her skills did not match her ambition: 'She does not understand the true character of the landscapes she paints, that her eye, indeed, only devours surface beauties, skin deep at best. Here, above all, a case can be made out for further study in the very rudiments of painting.' Broadhurst did not keep a clipping of this review.

She toured her paintings to Finney's Art Gallery in Brisbane, Anthony Hordern & Sons Art Gallery in Sydney, and the Masonic Hall in Bathurst, and appeared in exhibitions with other, more noted, artists such as Judy Cassab and Roland Wakelin. Broadhurst also unsuccessfully entered a series of fiercely competitive art prizes (the Sulman in 1958, the Archibald in 1963 and 1967, and the Wynne in 1965) but it quickly became clear that her world tour was falling through.

Broadhurst simply changed tack. She began to focus her unflagging energy more acutely on public speaking and the networking that could be done by involving herself in high-society fundraising. She found a use for her son, who is pictured in the *Daily Mirror* of Monday 22 October 1956 rock 'n' rolling with his mother. In the article,

*The illusion of dimension in **Pyramids** [opposite], printed on silver wallpaper, is created with negative space and stipple tones.*

COURTESY SIGNATURE PRINTS

60

she is described as 'the president of the dance committee' for the Royal Art Society's spring dance.

The RAS was a good organisation to be associated with, its members including painters of the highest order. It was expanding and in 1956 it used cash to buy two adjoining Victorian terrace houses in Walker Street, North Sydney, which remain its headquarters to this day. Most of the money came from art sales but it is entirely possible that Broadhurst's event also chipped in.

Sadly for Florence the artist, much of the hype ended here. She does not appear in the RAS's records as either an exhibiting member of the society or, indeed, as a member at all. Her quest to become the country's ambassadress also ended with little to show for it, despite her making it a feature of the United Nation's International Ball. Broadhurst was working hard but success continued to elude her. Then the most extraordinary thing happened.

On 14 February 1958, the Queen Mother began a three-week tour of Australia. Ten days later, she visited the Trocadero in Sydney's George Street as the guest of a women's reception at which dignitaries such as the New South Wales premier's wife and the Attorney-General's wife were in attendance.

Royal fever gripped Sydney. Local newspapers described wild scenes as over 2000 women surged through barricades and past police in an attempt to see the lone royal, shouting, 'Give us a fair go, coppers' and 'all we want is a view of the Queen Mother'.

Amazingly, Florence Broadhurst was already inside, one of around 800 women representing 150 different organisations. As the Queen Mother mingled, she would have been assisted by a local aide – standard procedure in such environments when the royals are meeting their public. Having quite possibly been told that Broadhurst used to live in London, the Queen Mother looked at the well-coiffed socialite and asked a question which would reverberate around Sydney's social scene for years to come: 'Are you living here now?'

Broadhurst did not miss a beat. She let those around her know that she had first met the Queen Mother at Queen Elizabeth's wedding and that the two women had spoken several times since. The timing was wonderful. Just a few months later, Broadhurst and her new found cache had become the star attraction of the Red Cross's fundraising Sydney premier of a British war film, *Dunkirk*.

The screening took place in an intimate city centre theatre, recalls designer Peter Travis, who watched the movie from the first circle with his close friend Phyllis Shillito, now regarded as a major figure in Australian design history. 'Florence, who was the president of the Black and White Ball, came on the stage,' Travis recalls. 'She had a black dress on with three tiers in the skirt ... She gave a twenty-minute speech on the meaning of Anzac and you could have heard a pin fall. She captured the attention of everybody. I don't remember the movie as much as I remember her. It was quite a moment.'

Broadhurst also agreed to discuss the impact of *Dunkirk* in the *Daily Mirror* (on 10 July 1958), and in doing so made an announcement. 'I've always been interested in charity work, but have only recently taken it up "full-time",' she wrote. She then went on to make one of the very few public references to problems with her eyesight that would plague her for the rest of her life. 'I made this decision after my doctor had told me I must give up painting for a year, as I was gradually losing my sight and the close work painting involves was hastening the process ... My impending blindness is due to the war. A lack of vitamins in my diet apparently created the condition.'

At home, too, things were changing. On 25 October 1958, Robert Lloyd-Lewis married Marlene Heaydon in Barker College Chapel, and took out a mortgage on a house in the quiet beachside Sydney suburb of Avalon. By the time Florence and Leonard became grandparents for the first time, Leonard had begun to develop what his son calls 'other interests'. He had a girlfriend only six months older

63

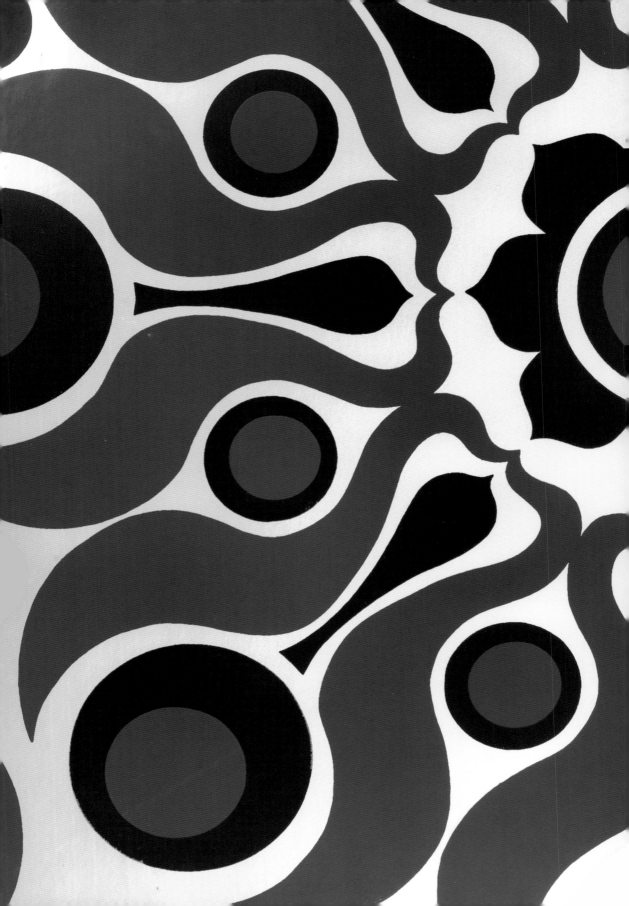

than Robert and this time he was not about to give her up. Leonard and
Florence's relationship was finally on the rocks.

Robert Lloyd-Lewis has one story from this time that he feels
encapsulates his mother's attitude to life. He had devised a business
plan involving organising credit, buying up trucks and starting a
delivery company. He talked his mother into visiting the bank manager
with him but the reception they faced was frosty. 'Who was I? Only a
bloody boy who had borrowed money to buy a house in Avalon [and]
oh and you've got a woman with you ... what does she know about it?'

'That was like a red rag to a bull,' he grins. 'Say "no" for any other
reason and she wouldn't have cared. Instead she said, "Right. What's
it going to take? We'll do it." So we acquired eight vehicles then built
that up until we were running a [large] motor company. We eventually
sold it to a company that became part of TNT.'

*Solar [opposite] in blue,
black and gold is a
seventies disco classic.*

65

COURTESY SIGNATURE PRINTS

As a business partner, Broadhurst was fairly eccentric. She never
queried figures, Lloyd-Lewis says, but she did want to know all sorts of
other things. 'Are all the drivers getting proper rest? They're not taking
pills are they? They're not damaging our vehicles, are they? They haven't
had an accident, have they? We haven't dropped a car, have we?'

'Sometimes drivers would go to sleep and come off the road, drop a car,
and we'd have an insurance claim. "You didn't ring me and tell me ...
you didn't actually tell me, you just gave me this little message. Old Vic
had an accident. Is he all right? How's his family? His wife? Have you
rung her? He doesn't have a wife? Why doesn't he have a wife?"'

Lloyd-Lewis understood that the business was not what Broadhurst
really wanted. 'It was done to help Robert the son,' he says. 'Our
relationship had begun to mature.'

What Broadhurst wanted was independence, in both a financial
and a business sense. She wanted a more public arena. In 1962 she
agreed to be interviewed for an article that contains her latest self-

transformation under the headline 'Artist braves the trucking business'. Leonard is not mentioned by name but Broadhurst manages to put a knife in by saying that this is her second venture in the field – 'the first time she let the business lapse for over seven years'. Her son is described as 'an experienced diesel engineer', and Broadhurst herself is a Londoner and a successful portrait painter who is quoted as saying that her real ambition in life is 'to beat a team of wharfies at a game of marbles'.

Buried in the story is a snippet that is all too easy to overlook. The previous year, Broadhurst lets slip, she started a wallpaper factory.

chapter three

CHANNEL 9 INTERVIEWER *You have someone here who makes the designs …*
FLORENCE BROADHURST *Well, I design everything.*
CHANNEL 9 INTERVIEWER *Do you?*
FLORENCE BROADHURST *Yes.* LATER

CHANNEL 9 INTERVIEWER *And you've designed all of these Miss Broadhurst, have you? How many of your designs do you do?*
FLORENCE BROADHURST *Eight hundred. There's eight hundred. You count them.*

The designer decades

Florence Broadhurst's wallpapers – vibrant, diverse and full of dynamic colour – opened a door to a brave new world. Gone was Bobby, the vaudeville vamp, who had been buried in a grave so deep that even friends of Broadhurst, such as the outrageous television personality Jeannie Little, had no idea that the vibrant redhead had once been a successful touring stage star. Vanished, too, was Madame Pellier, the elegant French couturier of pre-war London.

From the ashes of these incarnations rose a phoenix: Florence Broadhurst The Designer. Between 1961 and 1977, Broadhurst released a kaleidoscope of imagery with an international edge into an isolated continent hungry for visual stimulation. Everywhere she had been, everything she had seen would come to find a reflection in her sensual, funky, impulsive design range.

Viewed today, the Broadhurst designs appear to demonstrate a remarkable awareness of 'Australian-ness' at a time when the nation was only beginning to come to grips with where its heritage lay. Equally surprising is that the venture seems to emerge from nowhere. It burst

The hip outlines of **Curly Swirls** *[opposite] are inspired by sixties pop art.*
COURTESY SIGNATURE PRINTS

*Broadhurst championed Mylar, a strong polyester-coated paper that look likes foil but is stronger, with a bigger shine. Signature Prints [above] import it from the same supplier Broadhurst used, to create retro classics such as **Horses Stampede** [opposite].*

70

onto the visual arts scene with the same exuberant boldness that characterises Broadhurst's iconic design *Horses Stampede*, in which a crowd of line-drawn animals threaten to flatten everything in their path.

Understanding just how this eruption of creativity came about begins with the story as it is told by Australian designer Peter Travis, the man who worked on the Speedo swimming costume. Travis believes a crisis catapulted Broadhurst into the wallpaper business. He saw this crisis, he says, when he and Phyllis Shillito became acquainted with Broadhurst after the astonishing public speech Broadhurst made to introduce the star-studded screening of the World War II movie *Dunkirk*.

To Travis, Florence Broadhurst appeared to be a high society matron. She had red hair, dramatic make-up, a deep voice and – despite her diminutive frame – a powerful personality and an aura of complete confidence. He associated her with elite socialites such as Lady Lloyd Jones, so when he and Shillito visited Broadhurst at her business he was utterly shocked. The company Florence Broadhurst ran turned out to be a truck yard in the north Sydney suburb of St Leonards. Peter Travis was horrified. He had assumed he would be visiting something much more glamorous.

The relationship between Broadhurst and her 'husband' Leonard also struck Travis as strange. Peter Travis witnessed Lewis being called 'Mr Broadhurst' by accident and shrinking into the background behind Florence's domineering personality. He seemed more of a shadow than a husband and Travis remembers Florence Broadhurst happily recounting how she would put him to bed with a TV dinner so that he would be out of the way while she concentrated on her painting.

Broadhurst herself came across as an utterly unflappable individual, yet one evening she telephoned Shillito in a terrible state. Leonard had run off with a younger woman and his desertion had left her with financial problems. What was she to do?

Privately, Travis and Shillito were not surprised that the relationship was over because Leonard Lewis had seemed to them so terribly insignificant beside his domineering wife. They later spotted Leonard and his new, much younger girlfriend on a date in the city and noted that, in her company, he looked like an entirely different person. 'Leonard was all dressed up like a young man and they had a white dog on a leash,' recalls Travis. 'It was the first time he was probably treated like a man rather than a valet, or a doorman. He was now Mr Lewis.'

The separation marked a clear end to the Broadhurst–Lewis 'marriage' and Broadhurst moved in to her own apartment in the bright harbourside suburb of Potts Point. But the pair had decided to continue working together at St Leonards and this, according to Travis, was why Florence was so upset.

She had rented out a shed behind her truck yard to a couple who had started up a business there, and she was intending to use their rent as part of her income. But the couple broke up and the partner who remained, while determined to make a success of things, was having trouble earning enough money to cover the rent.

This was when Broadhurst rang Phyllis Shillito, who responded by going to visit her. According to Travis, who went too, Broadhurst was absolutely broken.

'I don't know what I'm going to do,' Broadhurst wailed. 'I have no money. I haven't been paid the rent. The boy can't work.'

'Oh yes, he can,' replied Phyllis Shillito. 'Look, he has a wallpaper business. What you do is help him ... get that business going. Then he can pay the rent.' Shillito lent Broadhurst some books on screen-printing, told her not to worry, and left her to it.

As Peter Travis tells this tale, his dislike of Florence Broadhurst shines through. He believes it is Shillito, a lesser-known woman who launched a design school in Sydney and trained a generation of designers, who deserves to be applauded. Peter Travis never saw

Florence Broadhurst at work but he holds an unwavering belief that she had no sense of design and that she was a talker, not a technical artist.

'If those boys had been making sausages – she was so desperate for money – she would have become famous for sausages,' he says. He describes Broadhurst as an 'opportunist' and a 'confidence trickster', adding: 'She would have made anything successful.'

Peter Travis's depiction of Broadhurst as a panicked, abandoned wife is persuasive and logical but is it accurate? Well, it dovetails in part with the passage of events as related by other witnesses, including Broadhurst's son.

Robert Lloyd-Lewis absolutely agrees that Florence Broadhurst became a designer by chance. The accident that led to it came in the form of John Lang, a shy, eighteen-year-old artist from Melbourne, who was renting a shed behind Broadhurst's truck yard. Whether Lang had a partner or not, Lloyd-Lewis does not recall. What he does remember is that the young man had got himself into serious trouble with Broadhurst for not paying the rent.

What was he up to in that shed, she wanted to know. Lang told her. He was starting a screen-printing business. The large, wooden frames she could see would hold the designs he had drawn. His long table was where he would print those designs onto high-quality, individually handcrafted rolls of wallpaper. These tones (showing her the inks) were the colours he wanted to print his images in.

Florence Broadhurst was not impressed. 'It's all wrong,' she snapped at the young artist imperiously. '*That* doesn't sell.' She found some bold, brassy colours and thrust them under his nose. '*This* is what sells.'

John Lang was not convinced and tried, lamely, to say so. 'But the colours are just awwwww,' Lloyd-Lewis heard him moan as he tried in vain to mount an argument against her. Broadhurst took over. As Lloyd-Lewis watched, his mother and John Lang spent hours

73

working together to create entirely new designs that seemed a world away from the sensible, subtle patterns that Lang had dreamed up on his own.

'She would say, "John this is what I want",' Lloyd-Lewis mimes, drawing a sweeping series of lines on a large piece of paper. His movements are quick, bold and decisive.

'She would make a basic outline with a crayon, a charcoal crayon. And she'd say, "That's what I want, but I want one colour there, another colour there, another there." "OK, so you want five colours," John would say. Then he would do it. He would draw the bits that she hadn't.'

The delicate sprays in **Spotted Floral** *[opposite] are rendered in deceptively flowing lines, offering a modern twist on patterns created by English designers in the late 1800s.*

COURTESY SIGNATURE PRINTS

74

Broadhurst took Lang's original designs and incorporated them into her new ones by printing them as backgrounds for those he created under her guidance. She used a well-established method of adding visual depth – the ghostly illusion of a third dimension – to otherwise static patterns on wallpaper.

Her vision was equally focused when it came to the question of who should buy these designs. Clearly, her clients would be the women with whom she rubbed shoulders at high-profile charity events. They would simply adore what she was about to unleash upon them. For if the upper echelon of the ladies who lunch would allow Broadhurst and her wallpaper into their dining rooms, women further down the social chain would want them too.

Broadhurst's timing was spot-on. Papering walls was all the rage – to such an extent that the word *pattern* was virtually synonymous with the word *wallpaper*. In Australia, a handful of companies were busy producing designs of varying qualities but the real creative playfulness was concentrated overseas – in Europe, which had centuries of images to fall back upon, but primarily in America. The United States was shoring itself up as an economic and technological powerhouse and an exuberant outpouring of visual creativity was underway. The building boom resulted in hundreds

of thousands of new homes – acres of blank suburban walls begging for some form of artistic individuality.

Wallpaper was perfect. It was lively, often cheap, and utterly disposable – as easy to replace as it was to select. Designers began playing with everything from traditional imagery to modernist abstraction. Extreme design collided with mass production, some wallpaper companies even turning to the work of high-brow artists such as Miro and Matisse in their quest for dynamic new visuals. Technology was changing, driving innovations such as foils and wipe-down walls.

Australia hungered for these funky new creations but the time and expense of importing meant that a fraction of what could be available ever was. To Florence Broadhurst the situation spelt opportunity. A new wave of colour and expression was ready to burst onto the scene. Hotels, bars and restaurants would lap up beautiful, functional new designs that had already become status symbols. People who were prepared to pay top dollar wanted to use them in their homes. The question was how to exploit that thirst.

The intricate, four-screen **Chinese Floral** *[opposite] has been digitally coloured from original artwork.*
COURTESY SIGNATURE PRINTS

77

In John Lang, Broadhurst had an artist. To make her plan work, she had to find a craftsman, somebody who could turn Lang's intricate drawings into saleable rolls of wallpaper. She got in touch with Sydney Technical College, wanting a printer, and they sent Peter Leis. The way he tells it, by then she was in fairly serious trouble.

Leis spent only a couple of months working for Broadhurst in the early 1960s. When he first arrived he thought he had the wrong address – he had been expecting an artisan screen-printing business, not a car yard. But there was Florence Broadhurst – outrageously dressed and theatrically made up. She walked him to a shed, where he saw one young woman hard at work painting designs in black ink onto pieces of clear plastic.

Japanese Floral, here printed in different colourways, is one of Broadhurst's most popular designs. For maximum impact, this design [above] is printed on Mylar.

He recognised what they were doing – making the artwork that would be used to create silk-screens from which wallpapers could be printed.

Leis got to work. Every now and again he needed to clarify something and would run along to the main office, where Broadhurst and Leonard Lewis worked, to ask a question. Broadhurst had introduced Lewis as her husband and he had seemed a normal enough chap. Until, that is, Leis popped his head around the office door to ask a question, automatically directing it to the man in the room. Florence Broadhurst did not let her husband say a word. She answered all Leis's questions for him.

The longer Leis stayed there, the stranger things became. Broadhurst 'divorced' Lewis every day. 'She would sit ... drinking tea or coffee in her nice little tiny compact office,' he recalls. 'Then she'd come down to the factory and say, "If *he* comes down here don't let him in. *He's* not allowed in. Don't take any notice of him. I just divorced him."'

*An original 1970s Broadhurst wallpaper sample – **Swirls** [opposite].*

81

She let Leis know she was a portrait painter and that she was terribly good at it. Her subjects were people with social connections. She talked, rather than listened, he says, and only heard what she wanted to hear. 'She *was* the most beautiful woman in the world. When she had her hair done it was brilliant – and she would have told the hairdresser exactly what to do ... Her clothes were absolutely fantastic. The whole day went on with this enormous flamboyance.'

Broadhurst used a powerful, portable kerosene heater to keep the factory warm enough to dry the printing inks, and she talked about it as though it were alive. 'Oh my lovely salamander,' she would say, using a generic term to describe it. 'Doesn't it keep warm? I don't know what I'd do without my salamander.'

Yet for Leis, all her eccentricities were nothing compared with the wallpaper factory itself. What Florence Broadhurst was doing flew in the face of everything he had ever learnt.

First came the question of registration. To print a design such as the classic *Birds of Paradise*, more than one colour had to be used. Each silk-screen held a different colour, so each one had to 'register' precisely with every other. If even one of the design's screens was as little as a millimetre out, the wallpaper rolls would not match up when they came to be hung on a wall.

Four-colour designs such as *Chelsea* were even more complex. The creation of *Chelsea* involved breaking up a stylised image of Japanese chrysanthemums into four screens: each of which appears abstract on its own. One has bold but confusingly incomplete outlines of flowers, leaves and broken branches; another the ghosted strokes of flowing stems. The final two complete the petalled flowers; one gently, the other with emphatic movement. Each piece of artwork has to match – or 'register' – precisely with the others, or the pattern is meaningless.

Birds of Paradise [opposite] – an unresurrected Broadhurst – features an arts and crafts inspired landscape.

COURTESY SIGNATURE PRINTS

82

Broadhurst's registration was a nightmare, says Leis, who was there when one client sent back boxes of wallpaper they had bought for the relatively pricey sum of £12 a roll because the patterns did not match up. The very next day Broadhurst sold the boxes to a department store for their window displays, for £14 a roll. Problem solved. Because the rolls of paper would be separated in different windows, the registration did not matter at all.

Leis only recalls seeing a handful of designs at that point. Broadhurst was concentrating on 'colourways' instead, selecting and mixing different tones to create different-coloured wallpapers which, when laid out, would look like an artwork by that other screen-printer, Andy Warhol.

Therein lay yet another conundrum, because Broadhurst wanted every colour mixed by hand. She bought big cans of paint in every colour imaginable, especially golds and silvers, and lined them up across a long shelf. When she needed to create a particular colour, she would find herself a small container and select tiny amounts of her rainbow

ingredients, mix them together with an electric mixer and – with a dramatic flourish – show the result to Leis. 'So what you had was this very fashionable woman who speaks with a plum in her mouth, divorcing her husband and selling trucks and whoooar' – Leis imitates the noise of the electric mixer – 'then she'd pick this [mixed] colour up and go: "Isn't it beautiful? [Now] you mix it up for me." And she would leave the room.'

Having watched Broadhurst move like a whirlwind from one end of the paint shelf to the other, Leis decided the only strategy was to do exactly the same, selecting random tones along the way and stirring them up to a rough approximation of the colour she had created. But what if that wasn't close enough? No problem, he decided, tipping Broadhurst's original pot into his mixture, stirring it all together, pouring a little of his creation back into her container and taking it to show his boss.

'She would go: "Oh that's lovely, brilliant." She had no idea. You started to get the feeling after a while that she couldn't see very well but then again she could paint, so it was hard to tell.'

Even at this early date Broadhurst was experimenting with spectacular new finishes. In the years that followed, she worked with a chemist to develop the vinyl-coated, washable wallpapers that were beginning to splash their way across the wallpaper industry overseas. Some technologies needed no improvement, though – she decided to import Mylar, the mirror-surfaced washable paper from the US, and print her own vibrant designs across it.

Leis witnessed the chaotic genesis of these innovations. He recalls Florence Broadhurst, who it was easy to forget was in her sixties, running up and down the length of her printing tables spraying her wallpapers with translucent golds. The effect was quite brilliant. It gave the paper a butterfly-wing, iridescent silk sheen – so that, as the viewer moved, the colour on the wallpaper actually appeared to change.

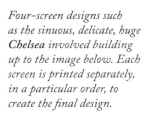

Four-screen designs such as the sinuous, delicate, huge **Chelsea** *involved building up to the image below. Each screen is printed separately, in a particular order, to create the final design.*
COURTESY SIGNATURE PRINTS

85

Controlling the effect was not easy. Ideally, whoever was spraying would put the paper up on a wall and spray it in situ. 'She didn't [do it that way] and each sheet of paper would never match. I could see that, but she didn't want to know. She was Florence Broadhurst and people liked her wallpapers.'

Broadhurst and Leis were clearly not a match made in heaven, and with orders for more wallpapers coming in fast, Broadhurst told him she needed a third printing table. He made it and she sacked him, for supposedly putting a bolt in the wrong way. 'She said ... "That's it. You have to go. Tomorrow. I don't want you any more",' and Leis walked out of her factory for good. He would bump into her socially twice more in years that followed but to him, she remains frozen in time; a bizarre eccentric whose success only makes sense if it lies at the feet of other people.

Counterchange [opposite], part of Broadhurst's 1973 wallpaper sample collection.

86

'I would always feel it wasn't her, that she had managed to attract the right people that could manage her and run the factory,' he reasons. 'She would be a nightmare to have in there anyway. Apparently one guy worked with her for about fifteen years ... Did he actually make it work and manage to control Florence? You would have to build a brick wall between her and getting the job done.'

In fact that 'one guy' did a lot more than that. Broadhurst could never have known it but showing Peter Leis the door changed her life completely. It left the way clear for her to begin one of the most unusual relationships in Australian artisan history.

David Bond was just eighteen when he started working for Florence Broadhurst in 1961, shortly after Peter Leis left. He describes himself with a halting shyness as 'a Barnardo's boy', meaning that he was one of several thousand children taken from England to Australia after World War II. He was – wrongly – told he was an orphan, and placed in care. Bond would learn that his mother was still alive and living in England many years later.

By the time David Bond spotted Broadhurst's newspaper advertisement, he had already worked at three other print shops. 'Mrs Lewis', as Bond called her, threw him in the deep end and during those first few weeks was so busy with the trucking business that she was barely there at all. Her artist, John Lang, popped in and out but Bond was basically on his own.

Pagoda [opposite] harks back to the mid-eighteenth century enthusiasm for chinoiserie, demonstrating a type of design often seen on oriental prints.

COURTESY SIGNATURE PRINTS

89

The place was a mess – too small for the amount of work Broadhurst was trying to produce and horribly leaky. When it rained, water dripped through the roof onto the printing tables, forcing Broadhurst to run around putting up umbrellas inside.

To make her business work, Broadhurst needed someone she could utterly rely upon, someone for whom having a job meant more than anything else. Bond, battered by years of being in institutions and fired with a belief that a job should be for life, was that man. He worked twelve hours a day, six days a week for Florence Broadhurst, ignored her flaring temper and laughed off her outlandish habit of literally pulling him away from his pub lunch 'in front of all the boys' if she felt there was work to be done.

When the harassed owner of a Kings Cross tavern ordered forty rolls of a two-colour design that he needed yesterday because a boat load of US sailors were about to hit town, it was Bond who worked two days straight while Florence Broadhurst fed him coffee and hamburgers, all the while telling him what a good job he was doing. Pounded to exhaustion, Bond grabbed a few hours' sleep on one of the printing tables only to be shaken awake by his irrepressible boss with the words: 'You stink, David. Have a shower. Then get back to work.'

'I never had days off,' he says with a sheepish grin. 'I tried, once, on a Saturday. I went out the night before, had a few drinks, stayed out late and slept in. She sent one of the girls around to knock on the door and get me out of bed to come to work.'

The way Florence Broadhurst saw it, there was no alternative. Sydney was changing and she wanted a place in the new order. The nation's other major city, Melbourne, hosted the 1956 Olympic Games but as the swinging sixties raged through the continent, Sydney was fast becoming Australia's international hub. Money flowed in on the back of the mining boom. Heritage buildings were torn down as modernistic high-rises sprang up to take their place, each containing endless interiors crying out for dynamic design.

Circles and Squares [opposite] combines Asian styling with simple geometric forms.
COURTESY SIGNATURE PRINTS

90

Things were changing at the Broadhurst factory, too. As the ever-respectful David Bond puts it, 'A few personal things happened up in the office. One day she came down and said, "I've changed my name",' he recounts. '"I'm Miss Broadhurst".' Bond did not know why, nor did he want to. 'OK, suits me,' he said, and starting the job of changing every logo on every wallpaper design from 'Australian Handpainted Wallpaper' to 'Florence Broadhurst Handprint Wallpaper'.

The cyclone that was Broadhurst threw herself into her work. Needing only four or five hours' sleep a night, she would begin her days at 6 am with two hours of portrait painting, then burst into her businesses well before 9 am. With one eye on her truck company and the other on becoming Australia's most prominent designer, she made sure that every one of her young, largely inexperienced staff was furiously busy drawing new images, printing rolls of paper and fanning the printed inks dry so their handcrafted wares could be rolled up ready for collection.

She created a catalogue bursting with images in everything from tasteful beige to the explosive colour schemes that reverberated

through the early sixties. A select group of interior design firms in Melbourne and Sydney would receive these catalogues, and they began connecting Broadhurst with clubs, restaurants and companies as well as her prized, wealthy private clients.

The sunburnt country's interior landscape had been dark and dingy. What Broadhurst wanted to do was inject the vibrant zaniness of the sixties into the veins of Australia. There were other wallpaper-makers about but none had her attitude or her energy. She worked as if she was on a mission: to destroy the drab and revolutionise the nation's palate, and she built a design studio that attempted to do just that.

Her wallpapers erupted onto the market at a rate that would have made William Morris's head spin. She attempted to cater for every need imaginable – from deep, red elaborate brocade-style tapestries that gave an air of sensual nonchalance to bars; through to massive, bold geometrics to intricate florals and elegant lattices so modestly executed that they seemed almost shy.

Parents who wanted to decorate rooms for their youngsters could select from a children's range that began with ridiculously naive line drawings of cats and mice, toddled through the semi-sophisticated Jap-pop *Pups* and the whimsical *Rabbits and Poodles*, and skipped into the evocative two-dimensional playpen of birds, turtles, dachshunds, fish, mice, cats and poodles seemingly inspired by the illustrations contained in 1950s children's books.

Broadhurst told a television journalist that she had 800 designs to draw from, although David Bond estimates that the final figure was closer to 550. Either way, the range is remarkable, in terms of both style and execution. The hand of her original artist John Lang, who created her earliest designs, remains visible in at least one image. Peer carefully between the delicate, whispery, curving fronds of *Small Fern* and you can find eight tiny letters that probably should not be there. They carefully – cheekily – spell out the name 'John Lang'.

*Broadhurst created the quirky **Rabbits and Poodles** [opposite top], **Cats and Mice** [opposite bottom], and **Pups** [above] for her children's bedroom range.*

COURTESY SIGNATURE PRINTS

93

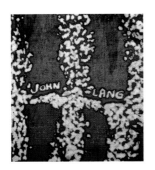

Small Fern is a gentle, traditional wallpaper with a secret. Hidden deep among the bracts of whispering fronds lies the name of its artist: Broadhurst employee John Lang.

COURTESY SIGNATURE PRINTS

94

Lloyd-Lewis describes Lang as Broadhurst's 'left hand' yet David Bond saw the quiet, self-effacing artist in the business only sporadically and recalls him disappearing for months on end. When Lang was about, Broadhurst made a point of mentioning his name to people, particularly to the press. That she re-hired him several months before her death made some suspect that he was the true creative powerhouse behind her business but, given the rate at which she rolled out new wallpaper designs in his absence, this could not have been the case.

So how did Florence Broadhurst do it? She had no track record as a designer, questionable skills, little obvious training and eyesight that made even Peter Leis wonder if she could see clearly. Turning abstract patterns into repeatable, attractive wallpaper designs is a very specific craft and certainly, by the late sixties, Florence Broadhurst understood the difficulties, at least, perfectly.

She explained the issues to European interior design specialist Babette Hayes, who co-authored the 1970 book *Australian Style* after hearing one too many times that the country had no style of its own. Hayes had moved to Australia from what was still thought of as the Mother Country, Britain, and she found herself intrigued by the creative ingenuity of those working in the arts. Australia was young, younger even than America, and brashly insecure. Ideas competed for cultural superiority: that Australia was white; that it was a British outpost; that if a notion originated in Europe it was automatically better than anything homegrown.

Hayes saw things differently. To her, the idea that any country could be a cultural vacuum was absurd. Australia was young by European standards but every country breeds its own identity. In arenas such as art and design, a fertile, formative debate was underway. It was visual, not verbal, but this was an argument nonetheless; a discussion in which creative individuals were attempting to define what it could mean to be Australian. Their deliberations were tangible – in the form of buildings created by Viennese-born architect Harry Seidler,

Broadhurst standing behind her desk in her wallpaper showroom, on the first floor of 12–24 Roylston Street, Paddington. The wallpaper factory was below.

96

the decimal currency designed by Gordon Andrews, and interiors by
the influential avant garde creative Marion Hall Best. Pioneers were at
work and Hayes identified Florence Broadhurst as one.

To Hayes, Broadhurst was innovative and forthright in her creative
vision. She describes the Australian design scene of the time as 'a wide
and lonely desert' because in 1970 there were no major design schools
nor any full-time design courses. Those wanting to make their mark
had to do so using stealth and determination.

Broadhurst fitted the bill. The story she told Hayes was that she was
English, having trained in Europe as an artist. She appeared to be
a volcano of creativity with hundreds of designs in production and
always 'another forty in mind', Hayes noted. 'Her ideas tumble over
each other faster than she can commit them to paper. She works at
a small drawing board under that peculiarly intense Australian light
falling from a window directly onto her paper and fashions her designs
with a dextrous ability ... Her papers have spread gradually all over
Australia until her signature is obvious in office buildings, hotels and,
more than anywhere else, in the homes of the nation.'

Wallpaper design required a precise combination of patterning and
mathematics, Broadhurst explained, in Hayes's book. 'One simply
cannot make an error. No matter how delicate and complicated the
design, there is no possibility of letting a mistake occur. There is no
tolerance at all because a mistake will be magnified a thousand times
once we begin to print.'

Hayes visited Florence Broadhurst's factory and went out to restaurants
with her. It never occurred to her to question the Florence Broadhurst
story, which the woman herself outlined in greater detail in a bound
copy of 'Personalisation Pays Off', notes for a speech by Florence
Broadhurst, circa 1975, which is held in Sydney's Mitchell Library.

'I began alone in 1959 with space for only two tables in a disused shed
at the back of a truck yard at St Leonards,' Broadhurst would tell the

97

crowds who came to hear her talk. In classic Broadhurst style, she wooed them with a tale made up, in roughly equal doses, of honesty, chutzpah and plain old lies.

'In the beginning, there was no pool of labour and each new member of staff had to be thoroughly trained by me ... My background is one of creativity – educated in art design and music, painting and interior decoration. In addition, my world travel from an early age helped me to become acquainted in all spheres of design.'

Australians were horribly conservative in their tastes. 'I realised that it would not be an easy task to persuade them to be a little more adventurous with the effects of bold colour and colour harmony, and in addition to try the effects of three dimensions and colour vibration as well as using metal papers and gloss foils ... Full of enthusiasm, ideas and hope, I set out to pioneer this new field.'

It is a wonderful, Churchillian speech, addressing every question without really answering any of them. It outlines Broadhurst's business vision, which is focused, sharp and unwavering, and ignores sticky issues such as Broadhurst's actual vision, which was problematic to say the least.

Robert Lloyd-Lewis recalls difficulties with his mother's eyesight becoming apparent to him before she moved her wallpaper factory to its larger, more upmarket location in Paddington in 1969. 'She never discussed her age, or her sight, or who she went home with last night,' he says, 'but I knew, and she knew that I knew because she would say "What does that say over there, dear?"'

When they went to a restaurant, the waiter would hand her a menu and instead of looking at it she would ask her son: '"Darling, what do you recommend?" In a subtle light, she couldn't see. If the spotlight wasn't sitting on top of [what she was looking at], she could not see,' he says.

For a lesser individual, the notion of passing oneself off as a designer when one had trouble even making out one's name in a newspaper clipping might have been reason to think twice. Not Broadhurst. Says Lloyd-Lewis, her general philosophy was, 'We will get by. We will go on. Life is full of challenges. We will accept them and go on.' So on she went, with such unassailable certainty no one, it seems, even considered questioning her about how she could turn out intricate, perfect designs when she could barely read a menu.

In the eyes of the world, Florence Broadhurst was a designer, and designers do not have vision problems. This was by no means the first time Florence had recreated herself but it was by far the most ambitious. To pull off a charade at this level requires strength of character, unwavering self-confidence and masterful misdirection. For it to work, Broadhurst had to do two things. She had to create an image of herself so vivid and powerful that few would even think to question it. She also had to keep a very tight rein over those close enough to suspect the truth.

Fictions can take on a life of their own. In his book *My Trade*, British journalist Andrew Marr tells the story of Phillip Knightley, who invented a serial molester called 'The Hook' while working on a Sydney newspaper. Knightley made up quotes from victims and police about the pest, who supposedly patrolled Sydney's trains looking up girls' skirts with the help of a coathanger. Following a series of exclusives, Knightley got a call from the police, who told him they had caught the criminal. He concluded they were trying to save face, speculated they might be trying to frame somebody, and decided never to invent anything again.

There is no evidence that any journalists colluded with Broadhurst, although they certainly looked no further than her official version of events. Her friends and customers were closer, but most of them say it never occurred to them to ask questions. If Broadhurst said she was from Britain, then of course, she was from Britain. She even fooled Babette Hayes, who really was from Britain and who says that the idea that Broadhurst invented her nationality never even entered her head.

Still Life harks back to the late-sixties trend of playing with shadows to give flat objects an extra dimension.
COURTESY SIGNATURE PRINTS

99

Equally, if Broadhurst said she was the designer, then of course she was the designer. Why would she not be?

Yet there are no notebooks containing Florence Broadhurst's designs in her own hand. Neither are there any scraps of paper that catalogue the evolving intricacies of her ideas. Did she really concoct a design business out of thin air? The truth can be pieced together, jigsaw-like, through the recollections of those who worked with Broadhurst in a business that broke new ground in more ways than one. For, despite what she liked to tell her public, Florence Broadhurst did not create 'Florence Broadhurst' on her own.

chapter four

*'I'm sure there would be no psychiatric wards if there was more art.
People who take LSD must be terribly bored.'*

FLORENCE BROADHURST, *AUSTRALIAN HOME JOURNAL*, FEBRUARY 1968

Backstage:
the Broadhurst factory

On 20 July 1969, Neil Armstrong walked on the moon. It was
a small step for man but an enormous leap for mass media.
Nerissa Bingle, who was nineteen at the time, remembers exactly
where she was when the news came through. She was with the rest
of Florence Broadhurst's loyal staff, creating fabulous wallpapers in
a tin-roofed shed behind a second-hand car yard in St Leonards.

Bingle loved the atmosphere. Chart hits blared out from the radio
and because there was so little space everybody, from the artists to the
printers, worked in close proximity. The floor could be dangerously greasy
from turps and paint, and the fumes were sometimes overwhelming, but
there was always something going on – people coming in, parties being
thrown, sudden visits by the posh, demurely hatted and gloved power-
wives that made up various high-society fundraising organisations.

Part of the fun was that Broadhurst hired her girls young, putting
ads in papers specifying that no experience was necessary. Bingle,
a keen art student whose mother worked with design teacher

*Turnabouts [opposite]
is the ultimate in large-
scale geometrics; each
circle is approximately
35 centimetres wide.*

Phyllis Shillito, had been seventeen when Broadhurst took her on. Sally Fitzpatrick, who became another of Broadhurst's key artists, was sixteen. Her family had just moved to Sydney from Adelaide, and she happened to drop in to a job agency during her summer holidays.

'There's this crazy woman down the street who designs wallpapers and she's looking for a screenprinter,' the agency told Fitzpatrick. 'Why don't you go and have a look?' So the young girl found the factory, knocked on the door and heard a deep, imperious voice booming out from between a pair of legs: 'What do you want?'

Broadhurst was bent over double, busy throwing rolls of wallpaper through her legs and into a corner. Fitzpatrick, who was struck by the image, recalls: 'She had this fluorescent-coloured, sixties crazy dress on and I could see the whole back of her panties, almost like tight shorts ... I was looking at this and her bottom and [her] orange shoes with the heels bent back because she'd been shlepping around.'

Broadhurst was less impressed. 'You're not going to be any good as a silk-screen printer,' she boomed. 'Can you draw? Where are your drawings? Go home and bring them back tomorrow first thing.' Fitzpatrick did as she was told, only to have Broadhurst look them over and declare, 'You have traced these.'

'I did not,' the offended youngster shot back. 'I have never traced anything in my life. My mother is an artist, she would never let us trace anything.'

'Oh, who is your mother?' Broadhurst wanted to know. Fitzpatrick told her. Her mother Dawn Fitzpatrick was a highly respected artist. Her sister Kate, furthermore, was an actress who knew everybody.

'You can start immediately,' Broadhurst said. 'If you make it through the week I will take you on, otherwise you are out of here. If you are any good I will pay you $18 a week.' It was slave labour, but Fitzpatrick agreed.

*The two-screen **Khyber** [opposite] uses dimension on an unusually (for Broadhurst) small scale.*

COURTESY SIGNATURE PRINTS

104

Khyber

Solar, here printed in yellow and red, is a two-screen design. The third colour, orange, is the result of overlaying the other tones.

COURTESY SIGNATURE PRINTS

Redhead Paulene Graham was younger still when Broadhurst employed her. She knew the minute she clapped eyes on the haughty designer that she had never met anybody like her. 'She just radiated energy,' says Graham, struggling to convey the magnetism of the woman who was dressed in skin-tight orange trousers, lime-green plastic shoes with little flowers on them and a striped orange-and-white mohair jumper, even though it was summer.

Broadhurst's fingers sported brightly coloured rings – half looked plastic to Graham, the rest fantasically expensive. Her huge false eyelashes were colour-coordinated with her flame-red hair, which was lacquered to within an inch of its life. Graham was so overwhelmed that she didn't even ask what the wages were. At the end of her first week she opened her pay packet and found $8. Her weekly train fare to and from work was $7.20.

Leonie Naylor, then Leonie Geyson, was another fifteen-year-old addition to the Broadhurst stable: a timid mouse of a girl who had just left school and only knew she wanted to do art. Her mother spotted Broadhurst's ad and chaperoned her to the interview, where Broadhurst talked at the pair in a room strewn with wallpaper rolls. Naylor says, 'I felt very intimidated but my mother liked her for some reason [and] more or less said, "Oh yes, she'd like that job", and that was it.'

Naylor's main duty was running errands for Broadhurst's head printer, and she says she still has a few bones to pick with David Bond. 'Once he sent me down to the cake shop to get a randy tart. I asked for it, I didn't know ... Another time he sent me to the hardware store to get a bottle of compression. I was only fifteen, I had no idea.'

These girls were by no means the only ones Broadhurst hired but they are some of those who lasted. David Bond recalls a never-ending stream of well-connected art school students wanting to work with Broadhurst but most left after a couple of days, something that Paulene Graham puts down to Broadhurst's explosive temper.

Many left the first time Broadhurst screamed at them, she says. Graham knew that this was not how her friends' bosses treated them but decided it did not matter because she was learning so much and because 'two seconds later she forgot and she was onto the next thing'.

Sally Fitzpatrick was so intimidated that she asked her mother to ring Broadhurst and say she was off to art school instead. 'Nonsense,' boomed Broadhurst. 'Absolute nonsense. Sally will learn more in five minutes with me than in five years at any art school. Send her here in the morning.' Fitzpatrick spent her first six months in tears.

Broadhurst got another staff member to show Fitzpatrick how to create silk-screen designs so that the registration was perfect. As soon as the newcomer got the hang of it, she fired the other staffer, leaving Fitzpatrick to deal with Broadhurst alone. Fitzpatrick managed to cope. She was one of five children in a high-pitched, theatrical family, she says. 'My mother used to tear my drawings up as a child and Florence was the same.'

The tables turned when Broadhurst told Fitzpatrick something she had done was all wrong, and Fitzpatrick finally bit back. 'I told her she was talking rot,' she recalls. 'It was the first time I had ever talked back to her and she just belly-laughed, turned around and walked away.'

'She said, "I was wondering when you were going to do that", and that was it. We were the best of friends from then on ... I realised that she was a terribly funny woman with a great sense of humour. As long as you did your job and it was a good job, you were okay; she just pushed you really hard. If you were sensitive, you could not be around Florence but she was wonderful.'

Part of Broadhurst's charm lay in her eccentricity. She would sometimes catch the train from her Potts Point home to the factory and would often dress quite outrageously even for that. One rainy day she arrived at work with red dye streaming down from her hair. She did not make that mistake again. On the next rainy day she walked

109

off the train in knee-high boots, a black plastic raincoat, and a white plastic-bubble swimming cap covering her bright red hair.

She could be frightening but she was also a lot of fun, say those who worked with her. Her studio and factory had something of a carnival atmosphere about them, and no one really knew what was going to happen next. As long as they kept their heads down, got their work done and ignored Broadhurst's histrionics, most of her employees were very happy.

But Broadhurst demanded a lot from her staff. She hired girls who had raw artistic ability and turned them into in-house artists who would spend their days at lightboxes, painting jet-black ink on clear sheets of plastic to create the images Broadhurst wanted. Most now have no idea how many designs they worked on or even, in some cases, which patterns they actually drew. Fitzpatrick recalls turning images around extremely quickly: 'Depending on what it was and how complicated, how many colour separations it had, you could get one done in a day.'

Floral Trail [opposite] as printed by Broadhurst in the 1970s. 111

The big question mark hangs over just what they were drawing. When Peter Leis spent his few months printing for Broadhurst, he saw her giving her artists large sample books of other people's wallpaper designs and telling them to copy them. The notion persists that Broadhurst did little more than create identical images of other designers' work. In some cases, Broadhurst certainly did create copies. An extreme example is Florence Broadhurst's *William Morris*, a beautiful, naturalistic, flowing stream of flowers, stems and leaves which is an obvious and direct imitation of the 1890 William Morris design *Pink & Rose*. Yet Broadhurst would only direct her artists to execute such a specific image if that was what a client asked for. 'If someone else had a design that might fit, we would do it, we would copy it,' says Fitzpatrick of the way she and the others worked. 'But it was never exact.' According to Bingle, and to the other young artists who worked with Broadhurst, one of her starting points was indeed the work of these masters of design, and she kept a library of the

*'Textures', used as background for bolder designs, added depth and sophistication to the final wallpapers. A texture design **Slub** [opposite] is combined with a second pattern to create **Shaboo Bamboo with Slub** [above].*

COURTESY SIGNATURE PRINTS

best international sample books containing designs from the likes of America's Albert Van Luit and Britain's William Morris. Other influences came from images as diverse as psychedelic record labels and conservative shoes.

But while Fitzpatrick has concerns about how close some of the Broadhurst images are to those of Van Luit or Morris, she agrees with Bingle, that copying for Broadhurst always involved customising. Broadhurst called it 'adapting' and what she adapted was the work of the best designers in the business.

She would come up with design rules, such as 'do things in circles because it relates to the body, and life,' says Bingle. 'She had this big thing about the circle. Florence used to say, "We start off as a circle, and life is a circle." She felt people would be attracted to designs that moved in a circle. She would tell us to design to that rule, to keep things flowing.'

Bingle, who drew many of the calm, collected lattice designs in the Broadhurst range, found herself incorporating elements from other designers' lattice images into patterns that would work in different scales, to suit the needs of different interiors. Broadhurst would direct her to put one pattern over another in order to create a third image that would become a new Broadhurst design. Or Bingle would enhance an existing wallpaper design by breaking up its structural elements and reconstructing them in three colours, for example, instead of one.

Another favourite technique that Broadhurst used involved placing strong designs over what she called 'textures' – subtle prints of clouds, waves, dots or hatching, which could be used as background for bolder designs, and would add depth and sophistication to the final wallpapers. These textures had to match up in all four directions and were impossible to copy. They involved handpainting thousands of tiny dots or lines, and Sally Fitzpatrick was set the task of designing them.

Fitzpatrick had watched her mother paint textures on her own artwork and had picked up a broad understanding of the principles behind it. When translated to a design intended for wallpaper, the rules became more complex: she had to keep the pattern completely uniform and be very careful to be even-handed with the ink. Too much, and the final image would have thick dots in the design. The registration had to be spot-on, as well, to avoid even a ghost of a line running across the pattern. Broadhurst was elated when Fitzpatrick finished her first texture, the artist recalls. 'She said no one had been able to do it successfully before and she considered it to be a very important paper to have in her collection.'

There were a number of designs that Broadhurst could not do without. A small section of her clientele wanted Australiana, so Broadhurst directed her artists to execute simplistic images such as *Aboriginal Rock Art*, and the rather more artistically successful *Cockatoos*. Another essential was the whimsical range of sweetly executed patterns that mothers could buy for their infants' bedrooms, an early example of which is *Cats and Mice*.

In every instance, it was Broadhurst who told her artists what she wanted designed and Broadhurst who would accept their work or get them to redraw it until she was happy. Her artists knew she had terrible eyesight but when she was standing directly over a lightbox, she could see what she was looking at. Some of them suspect that she spent time when nobody else was in the office, making sure that she knew exactly what her staff had done.

Her diminishing vision brought a bonus. Her eyesight had not been very strong when she first got together with John Lang, and this is one of the reasons why she insisted on such bright, bold, dynamic colour ranges, according to Robert Lloyd-Lewis, who found even those very first designs 'horribly bright'. He says they were wishy-washy compared with what she created later.

Aboriginal Rock Art [opposite] reinterprets cave paintings and blows them out of all proportion. This image is of Broadhurst's original pre-screen artwork.
COURTESY SIGNATURE PRINTS

115

116

Cockatoos *combines a shadow-play pattern with tropical birds full of personality.*

Certainly, the images that emerged from the Broadhurst wallpaper studio as the years passed became emphatically more striking. That trend was definitely propelled by Broadhurst's failing eyes, says her son. 'That is why [the colours] were so far out. It was her eyesight driving her. "I want it brighter, I want it stronger. I want to *see* it".'

With her girl-artists working as her hands, Broadhurst turned to others to crystallise her creative vision. She needed another kind of brain: one that understood the cultural temperature, one that could push artistic limits in every direction.

118

She befriended several of Sydney's interior decorators, an energetic group that included Leslie Walford, Barry Little and Yvan Méthot. Each had different clients, different backgrounds, different attitudes and very different tastes but all of them loved what Florence Broadhurst could provide.

Today, high-end creatives such as Leslie Walford can get what they need when they want it, but in the late 1950s and 1960s Walford lived in a world of scarcity. 'Order wallpaper from a top international designer and your client would wait up to three months for it to reach Sydney by boat,' he says with a sigh. Broadhurst could provide it in just a few days. That is not to say he got her to copy what was available overseas, he adds quickly. 'There were lots and lots of sample books around ... but many of them were not very imaginative, not very good taste from my point of view. Using Florence I could change the taste, change the direction.'

To Walford's mind, Australia lacked classicism. Although Australian-born, he had spent his childhood in England, and studied at Oxford University and in Paris before becoming an interior designer in Sydney where he championed European sophistication and an elegant, subdued, old-school charm.

Australia was a mishmash visually and culturally, he says, and Sydney was verging on becoming a disaster, a cityscape in which all sorts of

strange architectural pieces had been added to and superimposed upon a history of rather simple Georgian architecture. 'I thought that there was too much mess and that it wouldn't be a bad thing if I avoided adding to it,' he says archly. 'I used classical ideas but I updated them and made them more suitable for Australia.'

Leslie Walford is the main reason that there are so many different versions of the lattice design in the Broadhurst collection. Broadhurst would get her girl-artists, particularly Nerissa Bingle, to experiment with creating new lattices that might appeal to Walford, print them up, then present them to him in the hope that he would use them. He did it so often that the printers started calling him Lattice-Leaf Walford.

The fast-talking Barry Little presented Broadhurst with a very different aesthetic. He, too, had a penchant for subtle colours and elegant design but his true passion lay in the enigmatic, complex art of Asia and the philosophies that lay behind it. 'I just loved the Orient,' he says, sitting in his Paddington home surrounded by beautiful examples of Asian furniture and art. 'It was in my blood.'

Little was not overly impressed with Broadhurst's early wallpapers but Broadhurst was determined to talk him around. She directed Sally Fitzpatrick to create thickly drawn, stylised bamboo prints knowing that Little would like them, and also ordered her to create images such as *The Egrets*, which would become an iconic Broadhurst design.

'*The Egrets* was probably an attempt to secure Barry Little. Flo was always wanting something new, with one interior decorator or another in mind,' says Fitzpatrick. 'We did so much searching through books, magazines, materials; the ideas came from all over the place.'

Broadhurst loved birds, Asian designs, Japanese-influenced materials, 'I am sure from her youth and time in China,' recalls Fitzpatrick. 'We did a lot of searching for something that we both liked, and then I would bash it out.' When the decorator for whom she was creating

121

Large Trellis Keyline [above] was custom-created for Leslie Walford.

The Egrets [above & opposite] was designed to tempt Barry Little and is now a Broadhurst chinoiserie classic.

COURTESY SIGNATURE PRINTS

the design appeared, 'she would have me get up from my art table and she would sit down with a paint brush in her hand and pretend she was hard at work. The effect was great: she impressed the decorator and they would then walk off to the end of the showroom, after admiring her artwork, and look at more of her designs at the end of the showroom.'

Barry Little and Florence Broadhurst began a creative association that blossomed into a long friendship and a series of whimsical, Chinese-influenced flowering-tree patterns. When Little travelled overseas, he collected mementos that interested him – scraps of elaborate fabrics and images of handpainted furniture that he would seek out for his clients – and brought them into Broadhurst's factory for her to see.

Scatter Daisy [opposite], an original artwork, stands out because of Broadhurst's generous use of white space and the random clustering of daisies.

COURTESY SIGNATURE PRINTS

122

Little recalls coming back from a trip to the United States with a wonderful, vivid pink design of large poppies which was perfect for one of his clients. He commissioned Broadhurst to recreate it in softer pink-and-grey tones with an added pearlised finish that she had by now perfected. The result was very subtle and beautiful, he says, adding that it was only possible because Broadhurst had the ability to interpret what he wanted 'perfectly'.

Broadhurst knew her design range needed to be as versatile as the tastes around her, and her friendship with the small, intense decorator Yvan Méthot paid dividends. Méthot was new to Sydney, a French–Canadian interiors specialist who had worked in New York and felt that his new home town was crying out for visual innovation.

In America, dizzying reflective metallics were sweeping in as fashion-forward designers turned away from the traditional and towards technologically based space-age trends. Called 'foils', these new papers were eye-catching and expensive. Méthot had already seen about 150 different foil backgrounds which raced across the colour spectrum in everything from gentle antique golds to vibrant, overwhelming reds.

'The papers were becoming very sophisticated [and] people like myself pushed them because they were such an innovation,' says Méthot.

Broadhurst loved stylised Asian
motifs. **Japanese Bamboo**, *printed*
here on foil papers, is a bestseller today.
COURTESY SIGNATURE PRINTS

Peacocks, one of Broadhurst's most
popular designs, featured in her
Roylston Street showroom.

Dropping his voice to a conspiratorial whisper, he adds, 'I tell you very frankly, the interior designers here didn't even know what a "foil" was. It was like pasteurised milk. That was why I was so grateful to have fallen in with her. You needed a lot of patience to cope with her but I had a very difficult mother so it didn't make any difference to me.'

Méthot wanted to experiment. Broadhurst took full advantage and roped him in to her 'design days' – Saturdays spent doing what Méthot describes as 'crazy things' with colours and patterns to create wallpapers she could put into her sample books. The pair would cut up existing patterns to create inspirations for new ones and mix up colours to experiment with. He recalls printing over twenty screens of different inks onto a single piece of paper just to get an effect, and even using a cheese grater on metallic foils to tear three-dimensional texture into wallpapers that would otherwise be flat.

Méthot also got involved in the creation of a design that became Broadhurst's most famous image – her huge, complex *Peacocks* pattern in which two fabulously feathered birds stand on a single, slender branch.

Broadhurst had noticed a trend towards pheasant images in the latest overseas wallpapers, he says. The idea was both traditional and timely, so she became determined to create a bird image of her own. In classic Broadhurst style, she decided to draw the exotic king of decorative birds instead of the humble British pheasant, and one day she showed Méthot a freehand, pencil outline of a peacock which he assumed she had drawn herself.

'I think she doodled it,' he says. 'She came to me and said, "Yvan, what do you think?" I ... said, "I think this is a clever idea", to which she replied, "But the head is wrong."'

So the pair worked the design over together. Méthot added details – 'I can pinpoint exactly which lines,' he says – and they kept at it until the image was ready for one of Broadhurst's artists to transfer it onto plastic.

It was complicated and difficult, says Méthot, explaining how the image was so large that, to make it a pattern that could repeat, they had to match the tail on one end of the screen with the bodies drawn on the rest. *Peacocks* had five colours in it, which meant five different screens. 'The detail on it is incredible,' says Méthot. 'We added all the time, all the different little idiosyncracies: a feather, a bit of a wing, a medallion. It became a very popular design.'

One of the first places where Broadhurst sold the wallpaper was a glass-fronted dentist's office near Bondi Beach, where the design – in bright purple, lilac and green – could be seen from the road. 'Everybody stopped to look at it,' laughs Méthot. 'The next thing you know ... all the dentists' surgeries around Sydney had bloody Peacock wallpaper.'

Yvan's Geometric [opposite] is one of the simplest of the Broadhurst designs that plays on line and dimension.

COURTESY SIGNATURE PRINTS

128

Méthot, like Little, loved to travel and when he visited the United States he would bring back samples of everything from papers to labels for Broadhurst. He pushed Broadhurst into abstract geometric designs, although he did not have to push very hard. John Lang returned to the business for a while and Bingle believes it was he who came up with Broadhurst's range of dramatic, abstract geometrics. Some, such as *Pyramids,* are almost Escher-like in the illusion of an added dimension and in their autonomous interlocking forms, and one, *Yvan's Geometric,* is even named after Méthot.

Walford, Little, Méthot. The historical graciousness of Europe; the alien beauty of Asia; the relentless technological thrust of America. Broadhurst gave each of her 'boys' the ability to realise their creative vision and her studio inadvertently became a distillery for the influences that make up Australian culture today. Many other decorators – creatives and non-creatives alike – used her factory, too, each bringing different stylistic influences to the table. Broadhurst's aim was to make sure that every taste, every whim, was catered for.

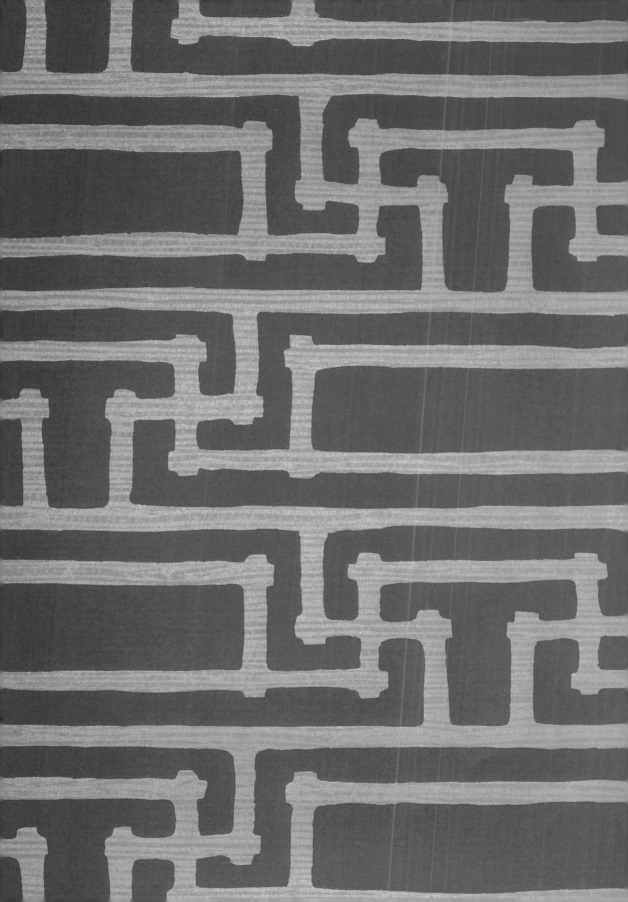

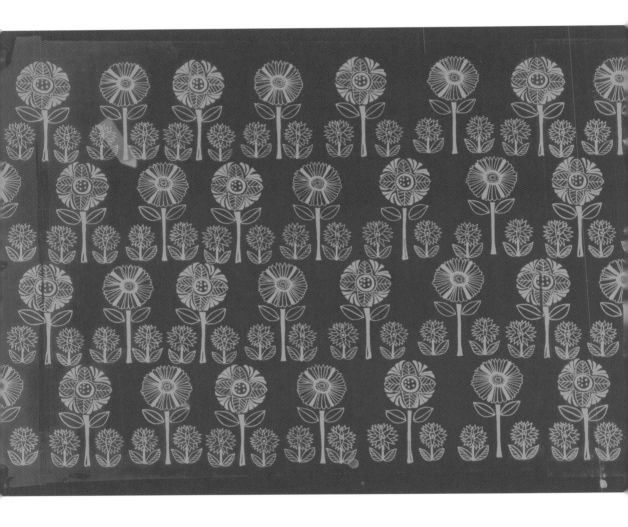

As the years went by and the number of fantastic patterns in the Broadhurst design range grew, David Bond, Broadhurst's head printer, became ever more critical. Described by those who worked with the pair as one of the few people who knew how to handle Broadhurst, Bond was the only employee she did not routinely scream at. If he did something she wasn't happy with, he would get the silent treatment for about twenty-four hours and then she would apparently forget anything had ever happened. Broadhurst needed him because, without his expertise, she could not fulfil any of her commissions.

Sally Fitzpatrick's brother Ben realised how difficult David Bond's job was when he worked with him at Broadhurst's factory in the late 1960s. Even at that point, Broadhurst was as 'blind as a bat' he says – her vision so compromised that much of the time she could not even tell who you were and would go around shrieking: 'Who's that? Who's that?'

Spot Daisy, *rarely used since Broadhurst's day, mirrors Japanese artwork with its flat, unmoving flowers.*
COURTESY SIGNATURE PRINTS

131

They worked on 25-metre, cloth-lined printing tables, using the same system with which Florence Broadhurst wallpaper is printed today. First, the paper was rolled out along the table. Back then, the paper was never perfectly flat – one edge was always longer and thinner than the other – so the printer had to identify which edge was long and then set stoppers along the length of the table to mark precisely where each screen should be placed. One millimetre wrong and the whole wallpaper roll would be ruined.

Then, the first screen was placed at the beginning of the paper. The printer took a rubber-bladed squeegee which was the width of the screen, grasped it with both hands and used it to pull ink from one side of the screen to the other. The printer would then pick up the heavy screen, move it up the paper and repeat the process until the entire wallpaper roll was printed.

If Ben Fitzpatrick put more pressure on one side of the squeegee than the other, the colour would change, because the inks were pressure-sensitive.

132

As well as printing on paper The Cranes, [top], Broadhurst printed onto fabric so she could sell curtains and blinds in matching colourways. The Cranes [above & opposite] has been printed onto hopsack basecloth for soft furnishings.

COURTESY SIGNATURE PRINTS

It demanded such focus that he and David Bond did not talk or even look up at anything else. Fitzpatrick describes it as almost like dancing.

'[David] and I used to work like mongrels,' he says. 'He was like a bloody robot. He would throw the roll of wallpaper down "Bang", then go up the table, putting the stoppers in "Slap, bang, slap, bang". He was so fast ... At the end of the day you would have done ten rolls, he would have sixty.' Every one of which had to be perfect. Fitzpatrick could not keep up with him, nor could he match the quality of the work Bond churned out. 'He was just too good.'

Every printer had a different technique, and the pressure-sensitive property of the inks meant that the colours would change according to who was printing the design. Sally Fitzpatrick, who also became a mixing specialist, got to know her craft so well that she could mix different inks for different printers. If Bond and her brother had to print the same batch of wallpaper, the final colours had to match perfectly, so Sally Fitzpatrick would adjust their printing inks accordingly.

There were other problems. Textures were very difficult to print by hand, says Sally Fitzpatrick. 'There were so many variances, like the weather (being a hot or rainy day) that the screens had to be stretched perfectly. The pull of the printer had to be exact every time or you would notice a difference in the thickness of the ink laid on the paper. It would show up like a sore thumb on a wall if the printer was having a bad day. David was a master printer.'

Demands from the interior decorators – particularly Yvan Méthot – pushed the craftsmen to their limits. Broadhurst wanted them to print on fabric so that she could sell matching curtains, blinds and pelmets; once, she even made David Bond print designs on glass. Ben Fitzpatrick recalls that handprinting Broadhurst's images on the imported metallic foils was nightmarishly difficult and virtually defeated him. It was only after a great deal of experimenting that even David Bond could turn out perfectly handprinted designs on them.

Working with Bond left Ben Fitzpatrick so adept at hand-printing that years later, when a Sydney clothes manufacturer suddenly needed a fabric that matched a particular, machine-made, five-colour design, because the overseas shipment they had ordered failed to arrive, Ben Fitzpatrick created it for him without having to use a machine.

'I could print fabrics to the standards of the best technology available, by hand,' he says. 'Unfortunately, as time went on the general feeling was "so what?". Machine manufacturers make it for 48 cents a kilometre and I make it for $160 a metre, so you are out of business,' he laughs. 'There is no call for it. Ultimately David Bond was in the same position. Our society doesn't support craftsmen or artisans ... Everything has been industrialised.'

Broadhurst wanted nothing of such 'progress'. She had no interest in swapping her craftsmen for machines. She kept hiring new printers, and one of her favourites was Neil Taylor – then an art student and now an internationally recognised painter – who worked with Broadhurst when he was in his early twenties until his painting career took off. He was one of the few she allowed to start work as late as noon – something he puts down to artistic philanthropy on her part.

She was more honest with Taylor than with many of her other staff, even admitting to him that she, like he, came from Queensland. The pair had conversations about the colour theorists with whom she said she had studied in Paris. She dropped the right names, he said, citing art teachers whose work was both valid and accessible, and every now and again she would open up some champagne and talk him through a photograph album that contained pictures of the bohemian life she led before she began working as a designer.

As her favourite interior decorators popped in and out, they began to notice that Broadhurst was always looking for new artistic challenges. To Leslie Walford, she seemed bored by the 'ladies from the North Shore' who would waltz into her factory dressed in their hats and gloves looking for ready-made wallpapers. 'She'd be relatively helpful but she hated them in another sort of way,' he says. 'She wanted more wonderful things to happen than just having these ladies match a little sample of something they had in their hand.'

'If I walked in there and she was looking after a gaggle of five housewives choosing their goodies, she would turn away from them, say "Ah, Mr Walford has arrived" in her rather grandiose voice and forget them to look after me.'

It is certainly true that some of the socialites who simply *had to have* her wallpaper had no idea what they were buying. Yvan Méthot says he sold thirty-foot rolls of Florence Broadhurst wallpaper for up to $270 each – over twenty times the price a normal roll of wallpaper would command – but it was when the glitterati had taken possession of their brand-new status symbol that the trouble would begin.

Pat Bryant, who is now in his seventies, is the son of a wallpaper hanger. He has two sons of his own who are also in the trade, he tells you proudly. In the 1960s and 1970s he worked for Beard Watson, the high-profile Sydney decorating company. Bryant was their paper-hanger; he cut, placed and pasted wallpapers everywhere from Admiralty House to hideaways of the ultra-rich and famous, and he remembers the era as one in which people wanted to stick their money up on their walls so that other people could see it. Broadhurst's paper was outrageously pricey but that was what people wanted. 'They wanted expensive wallpaper, expensive cars, expensive clothes. They wanted to show their wealth.'

Bryant became accustomed to the eccentricities of the wealthy. The first time that he wallpapered the Fairfax family mansion, he met an 'old bloke dressed like one of the gardeners [who] asked whether he could have a cuppa with me'. Bryant made him go and get his own mug, 'and after we'd had our billy tea I asked him what the owners were like. He said, "She's a darling but watch out for the old bugger, Fairfax himself." I said, "Why?" and he said, "Well, he's a bit of a tyrant." I said, "Thanks for letting me know."'

*Floral 100 echoes nature's
imperfections to give
visual softness.*
COURTESY SIGNATURE PRINTS

136

'Then he laughed, "I'm Mr Fairfax", he said. I nearly fell off my chair.
I ended up doing all their work for them after that, though. A lot of
work it was, as well. Mr Fairfax always asked for me.'

The first time that Bryant met Broadhurst is burnt into his brain with
equal clarity. He was papering a graphic, heavy-weave, gold-on-cream
wallpaper in a wealthy socialite's home and it was proving hideously
hard to hang. In all his years in the business, he had never come across
paper like it. None of the lovingly made, beautifully coloured rolls of
wallpaper matched up.

'There was a selvage on it like fabric,' he says. 'What we had to do was
trim that selvage off by hand before we hung the paper. Unfortunately,
when Florence was doing the printing she'd [leave] a half-inch margin
there, then a three-quarter, then an inch. In other words you could
not cut a straight line. So there [had to be] a certain amount of mis-
matching, otherwise you would end up with a white stripe running
down the wall.'

Bryant did his best, but halfway through the lady of the house started
to complain. He rang up his boss, who appeared thirty minutes later
with Florence Broadhurst in tow. As Bryant describes what happened
next the measured, good-natured tone of his voice rises, mimicking
that of a haughty individual who sounds absolutely assured that she
will get her own way.

'She looked at the paper and she looked at me. She said, "You have
done a very good job. I am very happy with your work". Then she
spun around to the customer and said: "Madam. This is handprinted
paper. It is *not* done on a machine. It is done. By hand. There *will* be
discrepancies in it. That is the beauty of *hand*printed paper. That there
are discrepancies in it. You can never copy it exactly. This can never
be duplicated. No one will ever have it as you have got it. You have
*hand*printed, *hand*-hung wallpaper. That is what you are paying for, and
that is *exactly* what is on your wall."'

'And with that she spun around and said to [Bryant's boss], "Can we go now?"' And away she went.

'The lady stood there with her jaw hanging down to her chest but she accepted it from then on. She said, "Now I think about it, it's true."' Bryant laughs. 'She even gave me a ten-bob tip to buy myself a drink because I had done such a good job.'

Some months later, Broadhurst invited Bryant to her factory because he thought he could provide a solution to her uneven selvage problem. He suggested getting a consistent margin by using a long piece of timber. 'It worked for about three or four months, then all of a sudden it stopped, I think because the paper was starting to look like a machine-printed paper. She was very keen on the handprinted look.'

And why not? Broadhurst's wallpapers were selling so well that even after expanding as far as she could in her old premises she announced one day to David Bond that she had acquired new headquarters at 12–24 Roylston Street in Paddington. 'Broadhurst said, 'Dave, come and have a look at this. What do you think we can do?', recalls Bond.

'But she had it all worked out. Truly. She knew what she wanted as she pronounced, "We can have eleven tables there, five tables there" – and this was just in one room ... I thought, "Oh boy, she's going to turn me into a robot."'

The Paper Makers, *Australian Home Journal*, 1968.

Photo captions [bottom left to right]:

1. *Cathy Asimus, Miss Broadhurst's chief assistant, is copying up a prototype of a pattern ready for reproducing on a silk-screen.*

2. *Cathy then colours the pattern onto the screen.*

3. *The pattern is printed onto the wallpaper by brushing the upper surface of the screen.*

4. *On particularly humid days, when the air is very still, the air must be disturbed above the paper to aid the drying process.*

5. *Silk-screen is being scrubbed clean.*

the
paper maker

IF you feel that the age we are living in is fa automated and uniform, then be thankful for the Flo Broadhursts of this world. Bubbling with enthusiasm new ideas and sheer love of life, Florence Broad has turned her unbounded energies to making printed wallpapers in a simple factory in a Sy suburb.

As far as we can tell, she is the only person in tralia to do this. Originally from Sussex, England, w she learned her art, Miss Broadhurst does her desi among the stacks and piles of wallpapers and fin designs stretched on racks to dry with girls fannin air above them. The papers and colors she uses specially imported from abroad; the papers from Sw and the colors from all over the world. These form basis of Miss Broadhurst's collection, but before s really satisfied with a shade she usually mixes the herself.

"I was once asked to print a carpet," she said. "It three months' research, and I had to get all the from the Orient to get the right shades."

All the technical aids for the production of printed wallpapers Miss Broadhurst has improvised h — drying racks, paint-mixing machines, and pri apparatus. It is because of this unique treatment that Broadhurst's papers are so individual.

"You get so involved with art that you lose trac time," said Miss Broadhurst. "And I'm sure there w be no psychiatric wards if there was more art. People take LSD must be terribly bored. I don't need it. I the more I do the more I can cope with.

"I haven't had a holiday in seven years, but I can switch off when I want to. I was once asked. 'How do know you are living?' and I said, 'I create, so I kn am living.'"

Miss Broadhurst designs to order, though she some standard designs always in stock, and they are added to every year as she gets new ideas and furnishing fashions change. "You have to keep a colle balanced," she said. The detail and color of Flo Broadhurst's work is really amazing. She has every from the most fantastic psychedelic patterns and colo the most traditional designs.

(Florence Broadhurst wallpapers are available from Pacific Highway (behind the boatshed), Crows N.S.W., or from Sydney decorators' shops.)

STORY/PENELOPE ROGERS, PICTURES/RODNEY WEIDLA

1. Cathy Asimus, Miss Broadhurst's chief assistant, is co up a prototype of a pattern ready for reproducing on a screen. 2. Cathy then colors the pattern on to the screen. 3 pattern is printed on to the wallpaper by brushing the surface of the screen. 4. On particularly humid days the air is very still, the air must be disturbed above the to aid the drying process. 5. Silk screen is being scrubbed

AUSTRALIAN HOME JOURNAL, FEBRUARY.

The grand opening of Florence Broadhurst's new wallpaper studio in the trendy Sydney suburb of Paddington was a big moment and her staff knew it. By the time they threw open the doors to Sydney's high rollers on 22 November 1969, the place looked spectacular. Broadhurst's theme for the Saturday night soiree was Hawaiian, and the 'flame-haired prima donna of the printing table', as one newspaper described her, wanted everything to be perfect.

'She was into psychedelic flowers at that point,' says Nerissa Bingle, who was told to create a series of new designs of 'wild flowers'. Bingle brought hibiscus blossoms into the office and drew stylised images freehand, from life. They were printed up into funky, multicoloured wall-hangings and used as decorations for the party, along with mirror balls and real frangipani flowers, which were scattered about everywhere. Food, a band, hired dancers and bizarre three-dimensional 'artworks' made out of tinsel and foils completed the picture.

140

Opening night at the new studio in Paddington, 1969.

Broadhurst decided she wanted a canopy above the grand entrance to her premises – something weather-resistant in an eye-catching, unique, semi-abstract flower print. It also had to have the initials F and B on it. Bingle took as her starting point the hibiscus design she had drawn, then stylised it again, incorporating a large F and B as they were drawn on Broadhurst's stationery. It was one of those occasions when Broadhurst was 'almost scatty' about the technical problems involved. 'The end result had to work, of course, but you had to work out how to make it work yourself,' Bingle says. All Broadhurst would tell her was that it had to be '*bold*. And *big*. BIG!'

The first night's invitation list glittered with luminaries of the social and arts scene. Department store heiress Lady Hannah Benyon Lloyd-Jones officially opened the studio in front of a crowd that included television's Maggie Taberer, newspaper columnist and social gadabout Nola Dekyvere, and milliner Countess D'Espinay. Barry Little took along his girlfriend Jeannie, who had made her own outfit from white fabric flowers. Barry Little says Broadhurst invited the social set

because they were good for business. Jeannie Little believes she had another motive. 'She loved all that. All the who's who ... She just loved looking the best there.'

Jeannie Little had the same outrageous sensibilities as Broadhurst and revelled in the fact that the older woman would dust her eyelids with wallpaper paint and throw parties in part to shock her conservative social acquaintances. Broadhurst was a 'wild fashion icon', says Little, who herself wore dresses made out of rolls of Broadhurst wallpaper and sported false eyelashes created from lace. The pair chatted about fashion 'a lot' she says.

Tortoiseshell Stripe
[opposite] experiments
with an organic notion
of vertical stripes.
COURTESY SIGNATURE PRINTS

The Hawaiian night was a hit. Sally Fitzpatrick and the other artists wore grass skirts and ended up dancing on the printing tables. It became the first of many bashes Broadhurst hosted at Roylston Street. She had a lot to celebrate. She had turned seventy earlier that year, although most of her staff believed her when she told them she was about twenty years younger, and moving into an arty suburb near TV stars such as Bobby Limb and Dawn Lake meant that she had arrived.

Broadhurst's new premises had a showroom upstairs and a large factory downstairs. This was where the craftsmen toiled: they mixed the colours, made the screens, printed the wallpapers and, if the client paid extra, waterproofed the wallpapers by spraying them with vinyl in a gloss, semi-gloss or flat finish. For them, these first three months were a nightmare because there was so much dust in the ceiling. 'We had a person standing permanently alongside me with a feather duster because all the sawdust ... dropped,' says Bond. He ended up having to dismantle the roof completely.

Broadhurst brought out new sample books and catalogued all the screens, already ranging from psychedelics to textures to geographics. The top sample books contained the full, 33-inch print of *Peacocks*, which was designed in a 'half-drop', so that the huge bird images ran diagonally across a wall. 'Magnificent,' says Bond. 'There were so many

colours that she put *Peacocks* in, it got belted. You could guarantee you were doing one order a week.'

Upstairs Broadhurst kept her artists busy. Nerissa Bingle remembers working on *Big Tree*, a massive stand-alone design in four colours, off and on for years until Broadhurst was finally satisfied. She had it put in the foyer, and David Bond recalls it as Broadhurst's personal design.

At first, the boss had her own private office where she received clients, some of whom were shocked to observe her rather Dickensian technique of employee control: throwing open a window above the factory floor and bellowing at her staff. Bond used to hear her voice booming out from high above: 'I can't see you, David, what are you doing?'

'Hiding,' he'd call back.

'Stop it,' she'd yell at him with a laugh.

She used the privacy of her office to good effect, says Sally Fitzpatrick, who would sometimes have a drink with Broadhurst mid-afternoon. 'I'd have a gin and tonic, she would have a Courvoisier, and we would get a little smashed together,' she says. 'Then we'd go out afterwards to some hotel in Double Bay that she liked to go into because they had her wallpaper in the lobby. She would walk in and talk really loudly about the paper "Fabulous, darling, wonderful wallpaper". Inevitably she would strike up a conversation with someone ... Everything was a sales opportunity for her. It was all about work.'

And work was rolling in. Broadhurst's designs would be hung in public places everywhere, from Sydney's Centrepoint tower to the majestic State Theatre, to clubs such as Tattersall's and upmarket department stores including Grace Brothers and David Jones. Ask David Bond for a client list and a 'who's who' rolls from his lips: 'Lady Fairfax, Lady Lloyd Jones, Lord Montague ... Lady Webster.'

By 1972, Broadhurst could truly lay claim to having international clients in Asia, America, Europe and Saudi Arabia. She had an

As eccentric as its creator, the two-screen design **Roman Soldiers** *[opposite], has not been used since Broadhurst's death.*

145

COURTESY SIGNATURE PRINTS

international reputation. *The Japan Times* described her as 'a dynamic, titian-haired artist'. Other articles about Broadhurst were published in the United States and United Kingdom.

Broadhurst combined business with pleasure. If she was off to promote herself at parties on a Friday night, she got Sally Fitzpatrick to glue on her huge, occasionally orange, false eyelashes. 'She would come back on Monday morning and they had peeled off on the sides but were still glued to her face,' Fitzpatrick laughs, adding that Broadhurst would tell her, 'I've had a *fabulous* weekend. Now fix me up.'

One Monday, Broadhurst announced that she was shocked. She had been on a harbour cruise with some gay friends and recognised an acquaintance who had been pretending, in public, to be straight. 'My God, you are never going to believe this, darling,' she told Fitzpatrick, roaring with laughter. 'That bastard, he's through.' 'I said, "Miss Broadhurst, you can't do that." She said, "Watch me," and she then sat on the phone all afternoon and called people. Poor man.'

Fitzpatrick recalls a series of toy boys that she says Broadhurst kept setting up in business. One was a builder who formed a partnership with Broadhurst whereby she would put her wallpapers in his new buildings and they would become a selling feature. One day she came in raging at Ben and Sally Fitzpatrick that something was terribly wrong with the artwork because the designs would not hang on the walls.

The brother and sister had a look and just started laughing because the builder's walls were six to eight inches off and the designs just magnified the problem. Sally broke the news to Broadhurst. 'I said, "Come on, Flo, look at this. It's not your artwork, it's the building." She just couldn't believe it. That was the end of him.'

Sally Fitzpatrick also remembers walking into Broadhurst's office only to see her bending a young man backwards over her desk. 'She looked up and said, "What! It's only Sally. Don't worry", and she continued on. He was terribly embarrassed, because he was putting this over on us that it was just a business deal.'

After a while Broadhurst moved herself into the larger space where her artists worked. She had a grand curved desk built and got David Bond and Ben Fitzpatrick to screenprint *Spanish Plate* on some glass between herself and the stairs so she could see who was coming up the stairs. It backfired, says Sally Fitzpatrick. 'People coming upstairs could see her but she couldn't see them. She would peer through the glass with her hands up trying to look through and they would see her doing it.' Broadhurst later installed a bell on the stairs so she could hear when people were coming up. Her staff quickly learnt to start jumping over that, as well.

Every now and again, someone Broadhurst considered special would come to the door. Judy Cassab, who is now one of Australia's most respected portrait painters, wanted some wallpaper but could not afford Broadhurst's prices. So they bartered. Broadhurst went into Cassab's studio for five two-hour sittings, and the artist swapped the portrait that resulted for enough rolls of a beautiful, gold-patterned wallpaper to cover the walls of her home.

The portrait by Cassab, which hangs in Robert Lloyd-Lewis's Queensland home, is both sensitive and strong: a muted portrayal of Broadhurst that seems alive with a captured energy. Cassab does not recall what they spoke of during the sessions. 'Every word my subjects say lands on top of my brush and gets straight into the face,' Cassab explains, but she remembers Broadhurst herself very clearly, 'and the wallpaper she gave me'.

Florence Broadhurst was at the top of her game, living her new role completely. 'To outsiders, she was the one doing everything,' says Nerissa Bingle, producing a folded, colour magazine article on Broadhurst from inside a brown leather photograph album. In it, Broadhurst is pictured sitting at a lightbox with a paintbrush in her hand. The picture caption quotes her as saying, 'If you don't do whatever you do with enthusiasm, don't do it,' and adds that 'sometimes [Florence Broadhurst] stays up all night to finish her work'.

'That was my desk and she's at it,' says Bingle. When the press came in 'we weren't actually doing designs, she was doing it all. That was what she made clear. We were just the dogsbodies ... It was all part of the facade.'

'She was very protective about keeping that under cover. Hardly anyone knew about it. Fair enough, that was her business. We were young, we never thought much about it, I suppose ... We were having a ball. We had free reign artistically, and it was very social ... the music was blasting. When you are that age you don't think much about the heavy things of life.' Bingle pauses. 'It was a good era,' she adds, 'Andy Warhol was a printer.'

Some of Broadhurst's designs suggest she fed off the raw artistic passion and the sheer sense of fun of those such as Bingle, who says that her work was probably as influenced by the likes of Jim Morrison's psychedelic record covers and the glaring colours of plastic laminated furniture as by anything else. Tucked in between Broadhurst's elaborate feminine images and her macho, intellectual geographics are some wonderful, throwaway examples of experimental anti-design, such as the huge, hilarious *Splashes*, quite possibly created by dropping huge blobs of paint from a great height.

Broadhurst made the most of inviting her clients in to what was a hive of artistic activity. She made sure her girl-artists knew how to sell to different people and how to charge them differing amounts, depending on how much Broadhurst liked them. If someone wanting to decorate a club was having trouble deciding, Broadhurst's advice was invariably, 'Oh show them something Spanish.'

Ben Fitzpatrick argues that it was the girls who were really in charge of the day-to-day workings of the business. His sister would take an order from someone such as Leslie Walford, match the colours to those he requested, create the design to the specifications he wanted, then get one of the printers to do a test-print to show to Broadhurst. At least once, after Broadhurst had rejected the initial test,

*Florence Broadhurst as she appeared
for the press. This is actually Nerissa
Bingle's lightbox.*

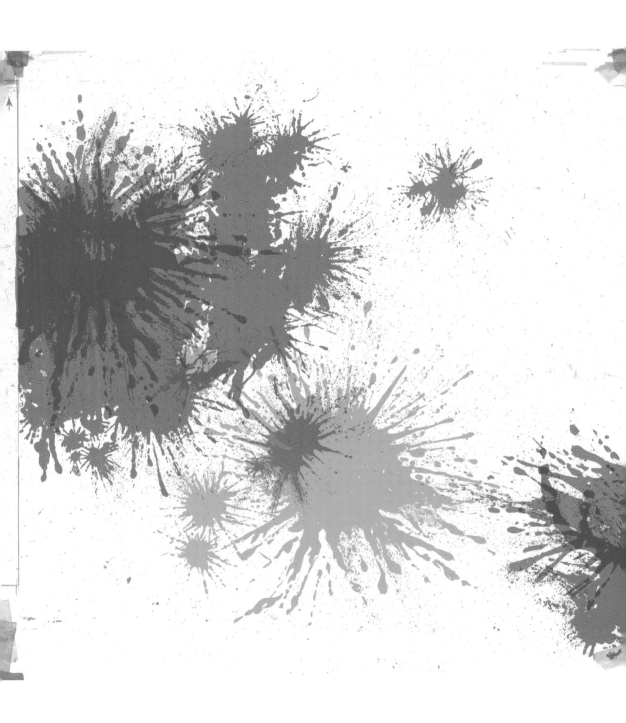

Sally took it downstairs, waited fifteen minutes, and took it back up again. Broadhurst said, 'Oh, that's wonderful.'

David Bond disagrees. His boss was in charge of the business, he says, and well aware of everything that was going on both inside and outside the building. She was very possessive of the public on-street parking spaces out front. If any residents used them, she would complain. Once, she even phoned the police. 'They said, "You can't do that",' recalls Bond. 'She said, "Yes I can. I buy tickets for the Police Ball." The copper looked at me as if to say "Can you tell her?" I just shook my head: "Nope."'

Broadhurst was clearly not to be trifled with. She was fit and energetic, and walked to work from her home in Potts Point almost every day. David Miles, who now runs an art gallery in New South Wales's Kangaroo Valley, did some work for her in the late 1960s and became embroiled in a dispute about payment. In 1969 he and his wife Cherie had set up in a wallpaper factory, David Miles Handprints, in direct opposition to hers. Later that year, the premises were broken into and trashed. Miles remains convinced that Broadhurst was behind the attack.

David Bond considers David Miles's accusations ridiculous, and of all Broadhurst's staff, Bond was probably the closest to her. Broadhurst gave Bond the stability he desperately needed. Bond went to Broadhurst for advice on all sorts of personal issues, including whether or not he should marry his girlfriend. Broadhurst told him he should, and he remains happily married to this day. Graham says, 'I thought that ... in some ways he'd latched onto her as a mother and he was the aspect of a son that she wanted. An obedient son.'

But Broadhurst had a son, Robert Lloyd-Lewis. Some of her staff from this era refuse to even discuss him. Others talk in hushed voices of screaming rows behind closed doors. They concluded that mother and son hated each other with a violent passion. But they had no idea what was really going on. In their eyes Broadhurst lived and breathed

Splashes [opposite] is a funky Jackson Pollock-esque explosion that takes the idea of using a splash of colour literally. This design has not been seen since Broadhurst's death.

COURTESY SIGNATURE PRINTS

151

her business. In fact, Broadhurst had a family life, and it was reeling. She hid the truth of what was happening as well as Mata Hari hid her secrets. She was not just a divorcee, whose partner Leonard had by now moved to Perth, over 3000 kilometres away in Western Australia; Broadhurst was also a mother and a grandmother, and unbeknown to her loyal staff, she was dealing with a staggering series of tragedies.

Robert Lloyd-Lewis and his wife had five children in quick succession. Two of them died of cot death, and the couple then lost another son following a car accident in which Robert's wife was driving. The effect on the young family was enormous. Lloyd-Lewis dived into his work unaware that his wife was coping by taking enormous amounts of over-the-counter drugs.

Anemones, an original artwork that has not been published since Broadhurst's day.

COURTESY SIGNATURE PRINTS

152

'She used to buy Codril and Relaxatabs,' Lloyd-Lewis says. 'She would have the children go to a different shop every day to buy them.' She eventually died of renal failure and Lloyd-Lewis blamed himself. 'Why didn't I know? Why didn't I find all these bottles of tablets that she'd been taking. Why didn't I grill the children and find out? Why was I so obsessed with work that I didn't see this writing on the wall?'

The compounding shocks catapulted him into depression. He started drinking a bottle of gin a day and stood on the brink of suicide. 'My one true love was gone and there wasn't anything else,' he recalls. 'My mother ... found me at the end of a bottle of gin and said, "Hey, you've got to climb out of here. Put the stopper back in, and think about this. You've got two children [they were ten and nine] and you have a responsibility ... You owe it to their mum to look after them. She has charged you with this responsibility. This is what you will do."'

'My father didn't do that. My mother sat me down,' Lloyd-Lewis says. 'She kept saying, "This is but a challenge in life. You have to go on from there." That was when I first started to realise that she had so much inner strength. What happened in her life to give her these cold, hard realistic values? That was her thinking about her past, I think. Whatever happened in the past belonged there. Move on.'

Lloyd-Lewis did his best, slowly. In 1971, he remarried. His new wife was a 22-year-old advertising account manager called Leonie Withers, a 'lovely woman who took on two children and ... was a tremendous mum to these kids.' Withers and Broadhurst got on well, perhaps because Withers represented a stable influence, and while Broadhurst clearly enjoyed being a grandmother, she would tell her grandchildren, 'Now listen darlings, don't call me "Nana" if there's anyone else around.' Withers also recalls Broadhurst being 'not happy' about her inclusion in a magazine article on women over fifty. She was well over seventy at the time.

Even at this age, Broadhurst had amazing charisma and what Withers describes as a fantastic energy. Her great sense of fun was never far from the surface and emerges in her brief appearance as a wicked old lady in *David and Pyewacket*, a little-known short film made in 1971. She showed no signs of slowing down and still needed only about four hours' sleep a night. But her son says she was clever with herself. 'She would hit a peak and [then] she was gone. She would lock herself away. Having planned all these thing she would ring everybody up and say, "Sorry, I've got to leave town", lock herself up in her unit and have thirty-six hours' sleep. Recharge her batteries.'

Even so, her age was catching up with her. In 1972, Broadhurst was diagnosed with sensorineural deafness and given hearing aids, which she concealed with her spectacular hair and strategically placed wigs. In a quest to fix her failing eyesight she took a number of trips to the Philippines and visited faith healers, then went to London's Cell Therapy Clinic in 1974, in the hope that they could reverse the ageing process. She told at least one colleague that she had three facelifts.

Lloyd-Lewis took to visiting her almost every Saturday at her wallpaper office, where he checked through her accounts. She was doing well. In the early 1970s she flew to Zurich, London, New York and Singapore, where she landed a lucrative contract to design wallpaper for the Raffles Hotel. In America, she was slowly developing

Ever the performer 155
– Broadhurst at the easel
[opposite].

an enviable network of clients, and she also made inroads in Bahrain, decorating interiors for the Middle East Hotel Chain.

As she travelled, she collected, bowerbird fashion – picking up anything that appealed and bringing it back to her studio. She made friends with people in design capitals such as New York, and persuaded them to send back examples of the latest, the newest, the most fabulous ideas and products of every kind. Large and small, every scrap and memento became inspiration for her work. On occasion, she would hand her girls a tiny piece of paper or fabric the size of a postage stamp and tell them to create a wallpaper design from it.

On one of her many trips, Broadhurst caught up with Sally Fitzpatrick, who had moved to Greece. Broadhurst tried, and failed, to persuade her to come back to the business. Even so, the pair had 'a short, crazy, fantastic time together', says Fitzpatrick. 'We flew to Rhodes and she picked the pilot up on the plane. She spent the next day with him in bed ... I had no idea she was seventy-three then. She was just such a naughty woman.'

But between Broadhurst and her son, the sparks kept flying. One point of conflict was her refusal to keep her business finances above board. 'She never paid tax ... never paid a dollar,' he says, appalled. Another sore point was her habit of keeping thousands of dollars in her wallet, which Lloyd-Lewis thought was daft. Broadhurst thought he should mind his own business. 'If I want to go to America tomorrow, all I want to be able to do is pick up my passport, walk into Qantas and pay them,' she would say, adding emphatically, 'It's mine. I've made the money. I've earned it. I can do with it what I like.'

She paid her staff in cash and habitually left her wallet in her handbag, and her handbag lying around in her office. Lloyd-Lewis tried to insist that there should always be someone with her in the office, or that she should put the bag in a safe. Broadhurst refused.

On 28 February 1974, that handbag turned her into a target. She was attacked in her wallpaper studio by a young man who came into her

157

*A sample print (known as a 'strike-off') of the delightfully graphic **French Fountain**. David Lennie printed this while trying to work out how many designs were in the Broadhurst library.*

COURTESY SIGNATURE PRINTS

office and grabbed it, making off with $1300. Broadhurst was left battered and bruised. The attacker was never caught but David Bond speculates that it may have been a casual employee who had a drug problem. Broadhurst refused to allow the event to alter her habits.

In early 1977, she told her son she believed someone was systematically syphoning money from her handbag. He said, 'Are you sure you haven't spent it?' His mother cut him to ribbons. 'Are you actually suggesting that I don't know what I'm doing?' she snapped. 'It was like pulling a heartstring.' Yet another row began. It was just how she was, says Lloyd-Lewis: 'A dynamic person who didn't suffer fools and believed that anybody that didn't agree with her was obviously foolish.'

'I would have always thought that this was my biggest fear. That someone would have come up the stairs [at the showroom] when she was on her own and sneak in behind her and grab the handbag,' he adds sadly.

'For Christ's sake, that bloody handbag,' he told her. 'You deserve to lose it.'

chapter five

'I don't think you fully appreciate the importance of illusion in life ...
Honesty is essentially a disintegrating force in society [and] the
progress of civilisation made possible only by vigorous lying.'

'I live in perpetual amazement at the gullibility of my fellow creatures.'

JOTTED IN A NOTEPAD BY FLORENCE BROADHURST

The last act

On Friday 14 October 1977, Robert Lloyd-Lewis visited his mother's
Paddington wallpaper studio to go over her accounts. It was not a
happy meeting. 'We had a run-in,' he says, a frown crossing his tanned
face as he sits on the verandah of his home in mid-north Queensland.
'It was purely petty. She had given a credit note to some people in
Caringbah. I said, "These people haven't paid and you have got to do
something about it."'

'No, no, no,' Broadhurst snapped at her son. 'They are friends of mine
and if they haven't paid there'll be a reason.' Lloyd-Lewis rose to the
bait. In his mind, delaying payment up to a certain point was normal
business practice but this had gone on and on and on. '"Buggered if I
know why they're not paying," I said. That was it.' He crashes his palms
together to mark the finality of the moment.

'She went off. They were *her* friends. It was *her* money. It was *her*
business. What the hell are you sticking your nose into it for?' My
mother was a marvellous orator. She had the ability to absolutely slash

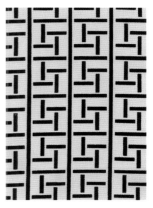

*These deceptively simple
geometric images are actually
two designs:* **Oriental
Filigree** *[above] and its
negative,* **Oriental Filigree
Reverse** *[opposite], both
printed here black on white.*

you into pieces on Friday and still expect to see you on Saturday. 'That was yesterday,' she would say. 'What are you talking about?'

There was a tacit understanding between the pair that Broadhurst would probably see her son and his family the following day. Not after this, she wouldn't. Unable to contain his fury, Lloyd-Lewis turned his back on her and walked out. He strode to his car, slammed the door and drove off with a single thought ringing inside his head, 'Buggered if I am going to see her tomorrow.'

*Bestselling author Dr Colleen McCullough has been a devoted Broadhurst fan for decades, using designs such as **Crocodile Skin** in her Norfolk Island home. 'I think she was hamstrung by being Australian,' she says of Broadhurst, 'She was quite unique.'*
COURTESY SIGNATURE PRINTS

'End of story,' he says, gazing into his weathered hands. 'It still eats me today that you can be so stupid as an adult over such a minute thing.' He mulls over the events that took place the next day. What would have happened if he had gone to see her? 'I live today on the basis of what would have happened if ...'

The following day it was business as usual at 12-24 Roylston Street, Paddington. Broadhurst arrived at around 9 am to find David Bond already hard at work downstairs with Alby Roberts, another silk-screen printer and cleaner. The rest of the staff were on their way in. It was a fairly typical Saturday. Customers popped in and out, looking, deciding, buying, while Broadhurst played host upstairs in her studio–office.

By 2.45 pm, things were winding down and almost everybody had left. Broadhurst gave Bond and Roberts their weekly wages and the pair wandered off to a nearby pub for a quick drink together before heading their separate ways. As they clocked off, they locked the factory's red back doors. At 3.30 pm, Wendy Soan, who lived just up the road at 27 Roylston Street, happened to notice some customers leaving. Ten minutes later, she saw Broadhurst close a first-floor window and pull down the blinds, as she always did in preparation for going home.

The police account of what happened next was first made public by journalist Valerie Lawson ('Blood on the Wallpaper', *the (Sydney) magazine*, 3 November 2003). Broadhurst walked into her kitchenette, a small room on the first floor that was hidden from the main wallpaper

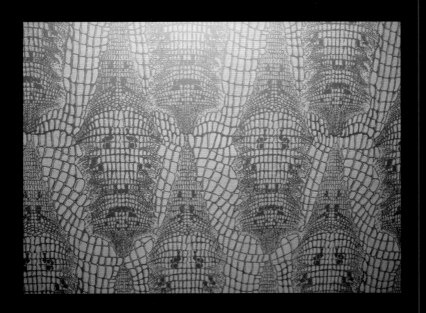

showroom by a curtain. She took some yoghurt out of her fridge, halved an orange and had a snack, leaving some uneaten segments of the fruit beside the sink.

Downstairs, someone came into the building via the unlocked front door. They picked up a piece of timber from inside the factory and made their way up the stairs. When they found Broadhurst in her kitchenette, they attacked her, hitting her nine times in the face and once on the back of her head, causing massive head wounds and fracturing bones in her skull, throat and sternum. As the 78-year-old tried to escape, her attacker forced her into a narrow washroom, and from there into an adjacent toilet where bloodstains suggested that she had been flung against the wall.

Broadhurst's murderer then carefully positioned his elderly victim's limp body around the toilet, shoving her head and her cardigan into the bowl. Her hearing aids lay scattered around the scene of the struggle and her fingers were broken. Two of her spectacular rings – one a 3.4 carat diamond and the other an emerald surrounded by ten diamonds – would never be seen again.

The killer went downstairs. Apparently familiar with the premises, he unlocked the back doors, pushed them shut from the outside, found the key used to secure the padlock on the factory's rear gate, unlocked it and then relocked it from the outside. The key left with the killer.

At 4.15 pm, three more customers came to visit Broadhurst. The front door was ajar, so they went straight in and climbed the stairs to the first-floor showroom, calling out to anybody who might be about. When no one replied, they wandered out.

The following morning, at 6 am, an elderly neighbour noticed that the Broadhurst business's front door was open and the lights were on. He alerted the police, who found Broadhurst's body and radioed for assistance from the homicide squad. Before long the crime scene was crawling with detectives.

Turnabouts [opposite] epitomises the importance of the circle to Broadhurst.
COURTESY SIGNATURE PRINTS

165

An unusual, positive–negative pair of images – **Shadow Floral** *[above] and* **Spring Floral** *[opposite].*

By the time Robert Lloyd-Lewis realised something was wrong, he was deep in a Sunday game of golf. His wife had agreed to caddie. When an urgent phone call came through to the clubhouse, she took it. Lloyd-Lewis's daughter was on the other end, calling from home. The police had rung. Something serious had happened. Her dad had to call them. As he did, a nightmare began: 'I couldn't believe that she'd gone. I couldn't believe that somebody who I ... had grown to love had just been snuffed out. I couldn't believe anybody would want to kill her.'

Lloyd-Lewis's father, Leonard, flew across from his home in Perth to be with his son. Together they identified Broadhurst's body at the morgue. 'They deliberately turned the body so that her good side was facing us,' Lloyd-Lewis says. He remembers barely anything about the well-attended funeral for his mother that was held in Darling Point on 20 October, five days after her death; nor too many details about the private family service that followed at the Northern Suburbs Crematorium in North Ryde.

Plain-clothed detectives mingled with the grieving crowd who attended Broadhurst's funeral in the forlorn hope of finding clues to the identity of her murderer. But it was her staff, not the police investigators, who had their eyes opened that day.

Leonie Naylor, now twenty-five, had worked for Broadhurst since she was fifteen and was sitting at the front trying not to cry; 'trying to think of the funny things that had gone on over the years ... I didn't want to think about her death'. As the minister outlined Broadhurst's life to the congregation, Naylor discovered that her boss was not English at all. She was born in Queensland, the speaker was saying. She had sung and danced her way through Asia. Naylor couldn't believe it. She thought, 'He has to be talking about some different person.'

Then one of the designer's friends stood up to address the crowd. 'They said, "Oh, she was a lovely little woman." And I thought that's the last thing she'd want anyone to say about her because she wasn't ... not at all. She was in a man's world really, a business person, trying to make her way, and ... in the 1960s and 1970s men really didn't take a lot of notice of women in business. In general, probably.' Naylor shakes her head. Her boss had forged ahead regardless. She had got the loans, built the business, made her name. 'She achieved what she went out after. There were so many other things that they could have said other than that she was a "lovely little woman". That was terrible.'

Sally Fitzpatrick was living overseas and missed the event completely. When she heard about it, she remembered a conversation they had had years earlier. 'Florence wanted no part of a regular crying and carry-on kind of funeral,' she says. 'Florence, Yvan Méthot and I laughed about it a lot. She wanted an Irish wake with three days of laughing and drinking Courvoisier, her favourite drink. We decided that we would all wear red wigs, plexiglass rings and orange eyelashes and we'd have a ball. She loved the idea. We talked about it for a few days and she made me promise that I would do it for her. It was never mentioned again but I still feel guilty about not doing it.'

Back in Paddington, Broadhurst's neighbours absorbed the news. Television personalities Dawn Lake and husband Bobby Limb, who lived a stone's throw from the wallpaper factory, heard what had happened as they flew back to Sydney from Perth. Says Lake, 'We were shocked to think that a thing like that happened so close to us, on a Saturday afternoon, in broad daylight. It was a diabolical thing. Terrible.'

The police investigation intensified. Leonie Naylor was among the many who were fingerprinted and questioned: 'They just went over and over and over stuff,' she recalls. They tracked down former employees such as Neil Taylor, who had worked as a printer for Broadhurst but was living out in the country at the time. Had he left under a cloud? They wanted to know (he had not, he told them); did he have an alibi? (He did not – 'In the bush, one day blends into the next a bit too easily,' he says. 'I really couldn't remember where I was.')

Yvan Méthot was able to tell the investigating officers that he was digging a pool at his home in Randwick with a friend when the

In later years, Broadhurst revelled in ruling the roost at high-profile social events. 'I thought she was the wildest woman, the most flamboyant person I had ever seen,' says performer Jeannie Little. 'Florence was electric. She was like a magnet.'

169

murder took place. The small, precisely dressed interior decorator shakes his head with disbelief, 'I couldn't believe it because I was supposed to have gone there that day ... They gave me a hard time,' Méthot adds, darkly. 'You only had to be a bit artistic in those days. I wore smoky dark glasses, long hair, mutton chops. I looked suspicious.'

David Bond came in for particular attention. To this day he remains so upset about the murder of a woman he says was a mother figure to him, and about his being treated as a suspect, that he cannot even bear to discuss it. Robert Lloyd-Lewis had to answer questions, too: 'I know for a fact that they checked exactly where I was. They did exactly the same thing to my father. I know at one stage they were trying to work out if he could have been here under an assumed name, then gone back [to Perth] again. If it had been an old romantic rift. They explored all sorts of things. They didn't leave too many stones unturned, but they never overturned the right one.'

All of the lines in **Milano Tapestry** *[opposite], here printed on silver scrim wallpaper, are drawn using hatching so the strong design does not overwhelm the viewer.*

COURTESY SIGNATURE PRINTS

170

While the police put out public calls for assistance, Robert Lloyd-Lewis and his father began to pick up the pieces. Broadhurst's will left everything to her son. His first dilemma was what to do with her wallpaper company. Sell up and get out, or carry on and keep the staff employed? Lloyd-Lewis and his wife, Leonie, decided to try to manage the business. Before they could begin, they had to deal with the mess that was Broadhurst's business: 'The finances were in turmoil,' he says. They had to work up deals to pay off the probate and death duties, which in 1977 made up almost half of Broadhurst's estate.

Hide your mother's jewellery, Lewis told his son, or the government will rob her. 'Just take it and put it away,' he said. 'Move it. They'll go through the house.' He also told his son to examine her apartment properly because he thought Broadhurst would have stashes of cash hidden away. He was right. Robert Lloyd-Lewis found two numbers which turned out to be safety deposit box details.

Lloyd-Lewis auctioned off most of his mother's paintings, which went for around $500 each. He acted on his wife's suggestion that they give

the proceeds to Phyllis Shillito's design school 'to help some young, struggling girl students ... get through their course'. He kept five or six of her works, including 'a self-portrait that my mother didn't like ... [and] one of an old bushman that she painted which is very much like my grandfather'.

Death taxes dealt with and jewellery squirrelled away, the Lloyd-Lewises dived into Florence Broadhurst's business. Some of it was straightforward; Broadhurst had just secured what turned out to be an enormous order from a Gold Coast high-rise developer. She would have been proud of how Leonie Naylor and David Bond kept the business going, he adds, 'with their dedication to my mother. Not to us, but to her. And John Lang. He was dedicated, too.'

It was very a difficult time. When Leonie Naylor left the business in January 1978 to have her baby she was glad to go: 'It was horrible. And you just felt that it was the end of an era.'

It proved too much for Robert Lloyd-Lewis. After two years of running the business that his mother was murdered in, he sold to the opposition. Broadhurst's remaining staff disbanded.

David Bond moved with the Broadhurst screens and artwork. Bond knew how to handle the eccentricities of those wooden frames, many of which were already warped by the ink and time that had washed over them. He was the only person who could get a perfect print out of every one of them, on any kind of paper a customer needed. But now that Miss Broadhurst was dead, his heart was not in it. 'It wasn't the same,' he says, his blue eyes welling up with obvious emotion. 'With Flo you weren't a number. With the other place you were ... and that's what hurt me.'

So David Bond walked away, the final actor to leave the stage. As he did, the curtain came down. That magnificent – unrepeatable – ensemble performance known as 'Florence Broadhurst' had finally come to an end.

chapter six

'I'll be there in a minute.'

FLORENCE BROADHURST'S WORDS TO SHERDENE ROSE FROM BEYOND THE GRAVE

Unexpected encore

When Broadhurst died, the mirror shattered. The illusion she had worked so hard to create fractured like a piece of shocked glass. Unable to pick up the pieces, and with the police investigation into her murder stalled, the Florence Broadhurst team moved on. David Bond, her printer and the backbone of her business, eventually moved north to Queensland to open his own screen-printing company. Her artists found new outlets: in motherhood, marriage and, in a few cases, other design companies. Her one-time design partner, the publicity-shy John Lang, crept back into the shadows. Robert Lloyd-Lewis was bitterly affected by his mother's unresolved murder. He buried his feelings so deep that after his marriage to Leonie broke down and he met the woman he would later decide to spend the rest of his life with, he did not even tell his new partner who his mother was for almost three years.

As the months went by, Florence Broadhurst's name dropped out of the public arena. She was remembered, if at all, as a larger-and-louder-than-life eccentric, a colourful individual who for reasons that no one could fathom had met the most brutal of ends. Yet while many were

Broadhurst's two-screened **Peacock Feathers** *[opposite] is a purely decorative design featuring highly detailed feathers that are drawn to life-size.*

COURTESY SIGNATURE PRINTS

trying to forget about Broadhurst, one woman she had never even met became utterly obsessed.

It happened by chance, two years after Florence Broadhurst's sudden death and cremation. Sherdené Rose, a recently married 41-year-old, had just moved into Broadhurst's Potts Point apartment. Within days, the self-proclaimed psychic became convinced that Florence Broadhurst was trying to communicate with her.

Rose started hearing muted murmurings, whispers of, 'I'll be there in a minute.' Rattled, she made an appointment with Robert Lloyd-Lewis at the Broadhurst wallpaper showroom in Paddington to find out more. She would later say that the moment she walked into that building, she recognised it from a terror-filled nightmare in which a shadowy-faced man with an earring and a battered hat was making his way towards an unsuspecting woman.

Lloyd-Lewis was a model of politeness. He showed the agitated woman around and answered all her questions, until she finally asked him, 'Why don't you have her story written?'

'Why don't you do it?' came his reply. So Rose tried. Never one to hold back, she became fixated, even claiming that she could hear Florence Broadhurst telling her to ' "write – write – write" … She was in my house – it was not my imagination.'

She turned her apartment into a monument to the dead designer, preserving everything from the showy silver and gold metallic designs running across the lounge-room walls to the silhouette of herself that Broadhurst had painted in her bathroom. Rose even kept Broadhurst's crimson-tinged boudoir just as it was; with its floral *Arabian Garden* wallpaper, matching curtains and custom-made bed, an extraordinary creation of hot-pink fuscia silk with a scallop-edged, half-moon canopy and a matching hot-pink headboard.

Broadhurst and Rose had much in common, she decided, before embarking on research to prove it. They had sailed on the same ships,

Arabian Garden [opposite], a floral with a vivacious swirl, is considered by some as one of Broadhurst's most compelling designs.
COURTESY SIGNATURE PRINTS

176

*Every wallpaper library contains a range of stripes. The more innovative – such as **Tortoiseshell Stripe** printed here in pink and blue – the better.*

COURTESY SIGNATURE PRINTS

178

lived in the same towns and both had relatives from the same English village, she would claim. There was some method in her mania. Rose obtained written permission from both Robert Lloyd-Lewis and Florence's sister Cilla to borrow family items such as Broadhurst's letters. Cilla, who was living in the Queensland town of Bundaberg, regularly went south to see her family in New South Wales and would occasionally fit in time to talk to Rose on her travels. In 1988, the coach that Cilla was in crashed with a goods train. The 85-year-old was one of two people killed.

Sherdené Rose never did get her manuscript published. It now belongs to her daughters, one of whom, Leeanne, also inherited Florence Broadhurst's vibrant pink canopy and bedhead. After attempting to donate it to the Powerhouse Museum, Leeanne decided to put it to work in the brothel she runs on Sydney's busy Parramatta Road. Her idea was a Broadhurst suite. Her rationale: 'A lot more people know about Florence Broadhurst than you might think. And if they don't know, I will be down there telling them.'

While Sherdené Rose was getting edicts from the afterlife, equally bizarre events were unfolding in realm of the living. Within a few years of Florence Broadhurst's death, her design legacy vanished so completely that it was almost as though she had never existed at all. Part of what happened was predictable. Fashions move on, and all interiors eventually come to grief. But Broadhurst's disappearance went far beyond the normal course of events.

Leslie Walford believes the timing of her death is partially to blame. By the late 1970s, the tyranny of distance that had separated Australia from the rest of the world was dissolving, largely because of the arrival of affordable air freight. Once, Walford could offer people perhaps three green velvets to choose from. Suddenly, they could pick from hundreds and have their choices within weeks. Florence Broadhurst died just as this revolution was taking place. 'Once she had gone, I think people weren't necessarily aching for what she had produced,' says Walford. 'She became more of a story [and] people have short memories.' But memories were something that the nation was trying to capture.

In 1982 a cultural flagship opened: the National Gallery of Australia in Canberra. John McPhee, the NGA's first Curator of Australian Decorative Arts, began scouring the country to create a collection that would demonstrate the breadth of Australian decorative arts and design. By the time he left the NGA in 1992, he had acquired a considerable creative haul, including the work of Melbourne fabric designer Frances Burke. Yet try as he might, he did not manage to locate any work of Florence Broadhurst.

McPhee, who says he has seen very few Broadhurst designs, is not a fan, although he does describe her as 'marvellously modern'. 'No one that I know who would have had a Marion Best interior would have considered going to Florence Broadhurst … The top of the range would have been Marion Best, whose rooms were very expensive to put together, and Florence Broadhurst would have looked more theatrical.'

There was a lot of money around in the sixties and seventies, he adds, 'and in Sydney a lot of flash trash … I regarded [Broadhurst's] work as being fairly derivative and not at the top of the market … That was my thinking, and that was the thinking in terms of the Department of Australian Art. She just looked like everything we'd all seen in London.' McPhee stumbled across a Broadhurst design much later, in 1997, when he bought a Sydney apartment that had been 'done over by Broadhurst', as he puts it. 'It had an amazing foil wallpaper with a lime green geometric print all over the top of it.' He could not live with the garish colour scheme and ripped it straight out.

'At the time, we knew about her but she had been murdered and the whole thing had gone dead. It was a case of not knowing who had the estate, who had the material … I don't know what happened but I never managed to acquire anything for the collection.'

179

What had happened was that Florence Broadhurst's work had become shrouded by the kind of web that only big business can spin. The threads began to knit together in 1978, when James Hardie Industries executed the largest takeover of a limited company in Australian corporate history, spending $52.1 million on the controlling share of Reed Consolidated Industries Limited. Reed owned a printing outfit called Wilsons Fabrics, and the following year, Robert Lloyd-Lewis sold the Florence Broadhurst business, and her Paddington factory, to a subsidiary of Wilsons called Signature Handprints.

Signature moved in to the old Broadhurst factory. It brought with it a creative treasure trove, the result of buying out designers across Australia and New Zealand. The acquisitions continued. In 1985, Signature bought out Donald Clark Associates, another design and screen-printing company, and its designer – Donald Bruce Clark himself – took a job with them as an artist. Once inside the Signature factory, then in the northern Sydney suburb of Hornsby, Clark saw hundreds of Florence Broadhurst silk-screen frames. These precious screens, once a licence to print money, were now just gathering dust. 'Signature didn't see any potential in them,' says Clark. 'They probably thought it was all passé.'

In a fashion sense, they were right. Wallpaper was on the way out. Restoration fever hit, giving Signature's craftsmen a new niche in the sympathetic recreation of heritage building interiors. But with the economic bubble about to burst, it was not enough. In 1988, Signature's parent company decided to break up the businesses.

New faces appeared in the Signature factory. One belonged to an intense bushy-eyebrowed New Zealander called David Lennie. Clark did not like the look of him, nor the way he seemed to be eyeing up the silk-screens stacked around the factory. Lennie was clearly up to something.

Clark did not know it but David Lennie had thirteen companies under his control, including a small Auckland handprint wallpaper company that he had bought from a husband-and-wife team in 1977, the same year that he visited Florence Broadhurst in Sydney. The journey to Sydney was a complete waste of time. Lennie got to Paddington, climbed the stairs to Broadhurst's office, explained who he was and found himself told, in no uncertain terms, to get lost.

Now things were different. Lennie was part of a consortium that wanted to buy Wilsons Fabrics. They failed; but, while sniffing around, Lennie realised that Signature Handprints was a treasure chest just waiting to be opened. He eventually orchestrated a buy-out and took charge of its piles of dusty, wooden silk-screens and boxes of film positives. He was delighted to hear that among the 4000 or so designs there were at least 112 different Florence Broadhurst images in the haul.

Clark, meanwhile, was in survival mode. He had started out in 1959 printing cork table mats and selling them from his home, and his own creative history lay inside another pile of wooden, silk-screen frames which were also sitting in the Signature factory. He was damned if he was going to let a stranger get his hands on them. 'I now have a shed full of my old screens,' Clark laughs. 'We ... moved it out so David Lennie didn't get his hands on them.'

But greater forces were at play than Lennie's syndicate could handle. Their plan was to float Signature Handprints on the stock exchange but the market crashed, losing Lennie 'millions'. 'I ended up with $10 in my pocket,' says Lennie, who went from being an owner of Signature to being an employee.

As the Christmas holidays loomed, Lennie picked himself up. He began a stocktake of the Broadhurst Library. He laid out every silk screen and tried to find the film positive or artwork that went with it. Not easy: none of the numbering made sense to him and some of the artwork appeared to contain little more than fragments of designs. There seemed to be no method to Florence Broadhurst's manufacturing madness.

Horses Stampede – *a maelstrom of repeated imagery.*
COURTESY SIGNATURE PRINTS

181

So he started the painstaking task of printing one image from each silk-screen onto a large piece of paper to see exactly what was in there. That, too, was confusing – some of the screens had no accompanying film and some of the film did not appear to relate to anything. Even so, Lennie realised very quickly that there were a lot more than 112 images in the Florence Broadhurst archive.

At final count, there were 530 patterns. The range stunned Lennie in its diversity and power. Particularly surprising was the quality of the artwork. Large-format designs are often executed with a cavalier carelessness. These were different: intricate, full of dimension and detail. Their sheer scale took his breath away. At a time when wallpaper was traditionally 52 centimetres wide, Broadhurst demanded artwork that was 72 centimetres wide – an increase in size of almost one-third.

*A block design alive with an almost three-dimensional feel, **Fingers** [opposite] is Broadhurst's take on sixties modernism. The largest fingers, printed here on a pink background, are almost 30 centimetres long.*

COURTESY SIGNATURE PRINTS

182

For technical reasons to do with arm-length, wallpaper designs that are going to be made by hand generally have a repeat length of between 68 centimetres and 75 centimetres, explains Lennie. Any less and the production rate drops, any more and the printer's hands are too far from their body and it becomes virtually impossible to create an even result as the coloured inks are forced through the screens. Broadhurst must have had the flamboyant foresight to instinctively know what happens to a design when you stretch the boundaries, Lennie reasoned as he leafed through the designs. She wanted big; she wanted bold; and she got it by forcing the width. 'What happens to the head of a tapestry design or a flower head or a geometric design when it becomes one-third larger?' says Lennie, 'This amazing visual opulence.'

Compounding the effect of size was technique. Lennie counted more than fifteen designs in which nothing but hatching and dots appeared. These were Broadhurst textures – background patterns to be used in a base colour which would add a subtle layer to a design without overwhelming it. 'These are probably the hardest artwork of all to get right,' he observes. 'Too strong and the base colour will take control. Too weak and the design-print colour dominates. Just right and the

visual result is like a perfectly cooked steak – sweet and tender. Today this is all but a lost art.'

Concealed within this huge pile of black-and-white images lay five so strong that David Lennie would come to argue that they be considered iconic. *Japanese Floral* contains flower heads executed with clever and careful line artwork and a print area that allows the shine of a metallic foil wallpaper or a silk fabric to make the flower head glow. *The Cranes* represented chinoiserie at its best. A classic design so soft and delicate that it appears to float above whatever it is printed on, it is technically detailed and precise but drawn with a free hand which allows the tree shapes to become very natural.

In *Peacock Feathers* lay pure visual madness. Within the confines of each repeat, confusion abounds. Nothing quite matches. In fact, says Lennie shaking his head, nothing even remotely fits. Yet the visual maelstrom works. 'All the rules in the design book say this should be a shocker but it is living proof that … going the whole way instead of chickening out can work.' *Fingers* is very different: a restrained example of purist geometric shapes. Another abstract, *Turnabouts*, is probably the best example of Broadhurst's belief that the circle is fundamental to good patterning. It was a favourite of hers and would become one of Signature Prints' bestsellers.

But all this was to come. As Lennie leafed through the huge pile of prints, he realised that he was only person who knew what was in there and that he was utterly powerless – nothing more than an employee. The nineties rolled on, and Signature ricocheted from one owner to another, each believing they could get Florence Broadhurst back onto the market and each proved wrong. Lennie was stuck in the middle – 'probably the only one who understood what was really inside this company' – and the turmoil took its toll. His nineteen-year marriage began to break down under the strain of his obsession, and his daughter Frances began a battle with anorexia that would prove fatal.

The Cranes, in detail on textured Mylar [above] and uncoated wallpaper [opposite]. The bird is one of the most important in Chinese art, symbolising longevity and wisdom.

185

Twice in that time, the Broadhurst library came under serious threat. In the mid-nineties, a Chinese owner wanted to ship everything off to China, and several years later a different co-owner seriously suggested destroying the entire archive because it was cheaper than storing it. David Lennie managed to talk him out of it.

By the late nineties, Lennie was back at the helm. He had remarried and his dynamic new wife, Helen, had a passion for Broadhurst that would prove an invaluable asset. Still convinced that the Signature archive was not only beautiful but important, he approached Judith O'Callaghan, the then senior design curator at the Powerhouse Museum in Sydney to see whether she agreed.

She did. Florence Broadhurst was one of many major artistic Australians from the fifties, sixties and seventies who were being totally overlooked despite having made a significant cultural impact, she felt. Until the 1970s, major institutions ignored Australiana, before that 'it was seen as junky and kitsch', says O'Callaghan, who now heads the Interior Architecture program at the University of New South Wales. 'It is only since then that there has been any kind of focus on local Australian production of any sort within design or decorative art.' Other nations understood the value of their creative output. Not Australia. 'In terms of, say, being able to go to university and study Australian design of the 20th century – forget it.'

The Powerhouse began a Broadhurst collection, agreeing to house the screens and artwork for Broadhurst's huge, dramatic *Peacocks* design. Yet getting Florence Broadhurst back onto the market was 'a nightmare'. Lennie had to find printers capable of dealing with the ageing, warped frames and the disintegrating silk-screens inside them. Some were so dilapidated that the designs were literally held together with sticky tape. The Broadhurst designs needed archiving and restoring, and therein lay another headache: a job of this nature required the time and expertise of a highly skilled artist.

'Nobody told me how hard it would be with no capital; really, really hard,' says David Lennie. 'I had been told by experts that this should be given a nice solid burial.' He ignored the critics. Florence Broadhurst had to have a place in the sun, he told himself over and over again. 'But it just kept on bloody raining.'

At 1.35 pm on 22 February 1999, Akira Isogawa walked into the Signature Prints factory. This was an important meeting. Akira, an introspective, Japanese-born couturier, was fast emerging as a major player in Australian women's fashion and his visit was a final attempt to solve a printing problem. He was creating the costumes for *Air and Other Invisible Forces*, an incandescent modern dance production due to premier at Sydney's Opera House, and what Akira wanted was diaphanous, net-covered robes upon which were printed 'inhale' and 'exhale' in Japanese calligraphy. Easier said than done. But after an hour at Signature, a solution emerged. Lennie invited Akira to his office. The time had come to test Florence Broadhurst on a professional.

Akira remembers the moment vividly. As he describes it, he is sitting in the corner of a busy coffee shop opposite his design studio in the heart of one of Sydney's rag trade regions, Surry Hills. Dressed in his habitual shabby black suit, Akira's large, brown suede shoulder bag sits at his feet, full of everything from hundred dollar bills to flight details – he is just back from showing his thirteenth clothing collection in Paris.

The designer has ordered a strong cappuccino to take the edge off his jetlag but the coffee is about to be forgotten as his mind wanders back to that first glimpse of Broadhurst: hundreds of designs printed in black-and-white on large, loose sheets of white paper. 'The paper was old ... it seemed printed many years ago,' he says. 'I had never seen anything like this.'

David Lennie offered no explanations: 'I guess he wanted to leave me to interpret ... without preconceptions,' says Akira, who did just that, assuming it was virgin, uncommercialised artwork. He leafed through

Helen and David Lennie.
COURTESY SIGNATURE PRINTS

187

Fashion designer Akira Isogawa showcased Broadhurst's **Nagoya** *[above & opposite] in his Paris collections. 'She is a very important figure in Australian design,' he says.*

188

the images, surprised to see such variety – abstract, art deco, textured, European. Yes they could represent the work of many hands but to Akira's eye they exhibited a single-minded, signature boldness.

This work was executed with an understanding of visual harmony, one of the marks of good design. 'Anybody can draw inspiration from anything but ... the final design should [have] that sense of balance regardless of whether the design is symmetrical or asymmetrical, regardless of whether it is monochromatic or colourful,' he smiles. 'It should make you feel happy.'

Two of the four-screen designs jumped out at him. The first, *Nagoya*, is a pattern of pendulous fruit hanging from heavily leafed branches. The second, *Chelsea*, is a fluid, dynamic pattern of long-petalled chrysanthemum – a flower that Akira feels expresses his childhood in Japan. He instantly began to visualise how he could apply these designs to his clothing range, in a rainbow of colours. At the back of his mind he noted that graphically they reminded him of the traditional kimonos his grandmother used to wear every day. 'Another design called *Fans* is heavily Japanese influenced. I feel really in touch with this sensitivity.'

Florence Broadhurst, he imagined, had hand-picked kimono textiles, as well as traditional fabrics she had found on her journeys through China. 'She would have spent time in England and hand-picked a Liberty print or something like that. Then mix all of that influence [to] create this empire in Australia. It all makes sense to me: the way she designed ... because that is also what I do.'

Today, the technique of cherry-picking details from the world at large to fashion new designs is well understood. 'I think Australia is a good place for this because it is far from the rest of the world. I see a lot of Australian artists, designers, who are able to view distinctive cultures, global cultures, with distance.'

Akira was about to show his first collection in Paris. He, too, would collect, bringing home mementos to feed his creative impulse. 'Based in Sydney and drawing inspiration from all over the world – Broadhurst was a catalyst for the way I work.' He immediately told David Lennie he wanted to use her patterns in his own design range.

David Lennie was blown away. Akira's reaction was his eureka flash: 'the most defining moment of what these designs really could be worth. Until then it was very much theory.' But he needed more than the imprimatur of one Australian designer. He wanted recognition overseas – the quickest way to bypass Australia's still operational culture cringe, he reasoned. Step one was telling a select group of interior designers (and one design store, Chee Soon & Fitzgerald) that he was bringing Florence Broadhurst back to life. Step two was marketing in earnest. Suddenly he was brought to a slamming halt out of the blue, by a man David Lennie had never even heard of – Robert Lloyd-Lewis.

The highly stylised Asiatic **Japanese Fans**, *printed here in soft colours, has a dynamic movement reminiscent of Broadhurst's* **Fingers**.

191

COURTESY SIGNATURE PRINTS

'They had no right,' says Lloyd-Lewis. As far as Lloyd-Lewis was concerned, he owned the copyright to his mother's work.

Heated words, lawyers' letters and tense meetings lead to an agreement. Signature Prints began paying Lloyd-Lewis for the right to market and sell his mother's designs. Articles about Broadhurst began appearing locally, but Florence was getting ready to return to the world stage.

In 2000, an invitation to participate in a British exhibition on Kiwi art landed on David Lennie's desk. It was showtime. He launched Florence Broadhurst in London, generating so much interest that Sally Ashburton, owner of the high-end London design store Borderline in Chelsea's palatial glass-and-steel Harbour Design Centre, offered to become a commercial international agent for the designs. 'They are exotic and striking, and very glamorous,' she says. 'They have an age-old elegance.'

British design aficionado Lucia van der Post, who later travelled from London to Sydney to view the Broadhurst archive, agrees.

'I was enormously impressed,' she says. '[They] have that timeless quality that all the best design has – and what I particularly like about them is that they have a personality, a certain zest and vivacity of their own. I think her designs will live on.'

Broadhurst's international profile kept growing. Selfridges department store in London began retailing ten-metre rolls of Broadhurst wallpaper for £160 each. One – a bamboo, printed in brown and gold, caught the eye of US film director Fenton Bailey, who sent his interior designer, A.J. Bernard. A.J. Bernard is now a die-hard Broadhurst devotee. 'I like the graphic nature of them,' he says of *The Egrets*, *Horses Stampede*, *Circles and Squares*, *Milano Tapestry* and *Yvan's Geometric*. 'Aside from *Horses Stampede*, which almost defies description, I find the others to be timeless designs capable of melding into any number of applications,' he adds. 'They have a classic appeal that works well in either art deco, modernist or contemporary settings but never seem to be kitsch.'

When Bernard discovered that Broadhurst was creating designs between 1960 and 1977, her range of styles made sense. 'That period was such a pastiche of everything that had come before, so it doesn't surprise me that her creations range the gamut from formal traditional (*The Cranes*) to op art (*Tortoiseshell Stripe*),' he says. 'In the sixties, there was a resurgence of art nouveau and art deco that carried on right through the seventies. Add in a bit of Warhol and Panton, and there you have it. At the same time, there was a desire for glamour and all things Louis XV and XVI ... I think Florence's patterns just helped bridge the gap.'

Back in Australia, David Lennie invited other designers to make applied use of Broadhurst designs handprinted at Signature. The result: everything from funky patterned rugs to cushions, bags and lampshades and Broadhurst-covered chairs. Broadhurst wallpaper

Modern designers are having a field day with Broadhurst, using her patterns across interiors, clothing and accessories [above and opposite].

COURTESY SIGNATURE PRINTS [OPPOSITE TOP LEFT AND MIDDLE]; FUNKIS [OPPOSITE TOP RIGHT]; GREG NATALE [OPPOSITE RIGHT]; KATHERINE [OPPOSITE BOTTOM LEFT]

began re-appearing in nightclubs and bars. Sydney's Ladylux nightclub used *Florentine Tapestry* in a vibrant red printed across metallic silver paper. Clothing stores such as Alannah Hill, Oroton, Mimco and Leona Edmiston became showcases for other fantastically flamboyant Florence Broadhurst designs, and innovative interior decorators began having fun with the range for their high-end clients.

Another early adopter was the Melbourne-based designer Nicky Zimmerman, whose women's wear is stocked in stores from Harvey Nichols in the United Kingdom to Bloomingdales and Saks in the United States. Like Akira, Zimmerman had never seen Broadhurst's work before, even though she trained in design and textiles in Australia. She had never even heard of Florence Broadhurst. Zimmerman also believes the widely ranging work has one single handler. Yes, the range is dizzying but it 'definitely looks like it has the handwriting of one person, even though there can be a print of a giant peacock bird and next to it you can be looking at a small optical geometric type of print,' she says. 'They still have a feeling, or a flavour that you would recognise.'

Zimmerman selected *Steps*, *Hibiscus* and *Aubury* to work with on her cheeky beachwear. The humour and the scale appeal to her. 'It's a bit kooky but beautiful,' she says. 'I think that is typically Australian – a bit wacky. There is a sense of fun with it. It doesn't have a serious feel to me.'

Tim O'Connor, a Sydney-based fashion designer, was also having fun with the Broadhurst range. Ever since he heard about the archive in 2000, he used one design a season and in 2003 he incorporated the striking *Bamboo* pattern into a collection inspired by the 1950s. 'I went all cream background and did a bright-yellow, very Liz Taylor-type dress with court shoes in bright blue plus a blue print on the white background with yellow shoes, and then a pink on white,' he says. 'It was very bling in terms of the colour. We also did a more commercial range in jerseys, and long dresses in a darker red on a pink and more tonal, not so in your face. It all just walked out of the store.'

*Sydney interior designer Greg Natale decked out an entire inner city home in Broadhurst's **Steps** [opposite], winning a Belle/Space Apartment of the Year award. Melbourne designer Matthew Butler took a flat-pack approach to Broadhurst, exhibiting his seat/table/boxes [above] in Australia, Japan and Italy.*

195

With summer 2004 looming, O'Connor decided to branch out and work with a much more delicate Broadhurst: the sparse, line-drawn *Butterflies*. 'I had chosen colours like lilac, watermelon colour, jadey green and had coloured silks dyed up overseas, which we printed on in a darker shade. It was a lot more subtle design-wise than the other Broadhursts I had used but the colours were pretty bright.' The experiment was doomed to failure, he says ruefully. 'It just wasn't that commercial.'

Even so, the range fluttered onto the fashion pages of newspapers and glossy magazines and, as it did, it fed into a bizarre and far-reaching chain reaction.

chapter seven

The butterfly effect

It was a Sunday morning like any other and Leonie Naylor was casually flicking through her weekend newspaper. Suddenly, she stopped. There on the page was a photograph of a chic dress created by Tim O'Connor. The outfit was made of soft, pastel-shaded material and it had butterflies floating across it. Naylor was sure she had seen that design before. Then it hit her. She had. She had actually drawn it years ago for her boss, Florence Broadhurst.

After Broadhurst's death, Naylor moved out of the city. She now lives in an idyllic, wooded spot north of Sydney, so far from any urban sprawl that the numbers of each house refer to how many kilometres they are along the winding, country roads. As self-deprecating as ever, she baulks at the idea that she created the artfully placed flutter of delicate butterflies that dances across the *Butterflies* design.

'Oh no, don't say it was mine,' she shakes her head emphatically. 'No, no, no ... Florence gave you a picture and you traced it. Or she might give you a picture and you'd trace it and alter it however she wanted.'

Butterflies [opposite] –
a gloriously spartan design.
COURTESY SIGNATURE PRINTS

But it was Naylor who drew that particular design image for her boss. 'Yes', she confirms. 'I did a daisy [design] and a butterfly.'

That Leonie Naylor was drawing anything at all marked a fundamental shift in the way Broadhurst was running her studio. She hired Naylor as an awestruck, softly spoken fifteen-year-old. Naylor learnt to print, mix colours and administer what Broadhurst called 'running repairs' – replacing Florence's false eyelashes if they were going astray and, if the boss had decided to come to work wearing an off-the-shoulder number, applying fake tan. Yet it was only long after Sally Fitzpatrick left in the mid-seventies that the shy, industrious girl was allowed anywhere near the artwork. 'I didn't have the knack for it,' she says, saying once again that she coped by doing something no one else admits to: tracing an image already created by somebody else onto a piece of paper and turning the image into a Florence Broadhurst design.

Fitzpatrick's departure had left a creative chasm that Broadhurst filled by bringing back her original designer partner, John Lang, but Naylor debates the notion that Lang actually designed anything at this point. She watched Broadhurst bringing in tiny images torn out of books, magazines or advertisments, 'and then the two of them would work together and ... put together a pattern'. Lang would draw it up, then they would play with it, 'cut it into pieces and move the pieces around like a jigsaw puzzle', says Naylor. 'He might have made suggestions but, as far as I could see, she was the number one and what she said went.'

The relationship between Broadhurst and Lang was love–hate, Naylor adds. 'I suppose he must have felt frustrated sometimes, because he was a creative person too but it just wasn't allowed to come through.' Lang would stamp his feet or go into the bathroom and slam the door and sulk.

In classic Broadhurst fashion, she told the impressionable youngster fanciful tidbits about her past. Naylor learned that Broadhurst originally came from Worthing ('not that I knew where Worthing was'), that

she was in her fifties (she was two decades older) and that during
World War II her boat had been used to go over to France and pick
up wounded soldiers, something Robert Lloyd-Lewis considers
unlikely as his family did not have a boat at that time. Leonie Naylor's
mother, Nancye, later wondered whether she had worked for Florence
Broadhurst, too. Back in the 1930s, Nancye worked in a Sydney factory
that made boxes for somebody called Madame Pellier. 'Big round
cream boxes like you might put a big hat in,' the elderly woman recalls.
'I remember the head woman saying that they had to be absolutely
perfect ... I wasn't even allowed to touch them.'

The coincidence got Nancye thinking. The factory's name was
Butterfield & Lewis – could this have any bearing on how Madame
Pellier came to meet Leonard Lewis in London? It's unlikely, but
there was one other coincidence that Nancye does not want to believe
changed the course of Florence Broadhurst's life. She sums it up in two
words: 'The wedding.'

In 1973, Leonie married Clifford Naylor, a 25-year-old British-born
man who had moved to Australia and swept Leonie off her feet.
Broadhurst provided material with one of her exclusive designs printed
on it for Leonie's wedding dress and she gave the youngster one of her
paintings as a wedding gift. She was invited to, and happily attended,
the wedding itself, as did the groom's mother Freda and her older half-
brother John Glover, who spent much of the reception chatting with
Broadhurst. Freda had just come over from England, 'so we were obliged
to invite them', says Nancye, who for years thought nothing of it.

On Monday 19 March 1991, all that changed when a police squad
stormed into an unremarkable suburban home at 14 Pindara Avenue,
in the quiet north Sydney suburb of Beauty Point, to arrest John
Glover. Head investigator Sergeant Dennis 'Miles' O'Toole had
no direct evidence but he and his team believed Glover was the so-
called Granny Killer, one of the worst serial murderers Australia has
ever seen. In the previous twelve months, someone had killed five

Abstract Butterflies,
digitally coloured from
original artwork.
COURTESY SIGNATURE PRINTS

202

Oriental Porcelain merges a floral design with oriental styling. Its drama lies in the deceptively simple execution.

Floral 100 printed in one colour on silver Mylar.

204

elderly women using the same modus operandi: frenzied violence followed by a cold-blooded, deliberate defiling of the body which was typically found posed in an obscene way. In each instance, the killer took a memento of his victim. He was careful not to leave anything incriminating behind. The public was scared and the press was having a field day with the police's apparent inability to halt the carnage. Finally, detectives zeroed in on John Glover and started following him.

That morning, at 10.26 am, Glover arrived at Pindara Avenue to visit a friend, 61-year-old grandmother Joan Sinclair. Nothing seemed out of the ordinary, so the police stayed in the background, waiting until 5.45 pm when a dog began barking inside the house. They forced their way in. Sinclair was dead, as viciously killed as the Granny Killer's other victims. John Glover was in the bath. He had swallowed every pill he could find in the bathroom cabinet, washed them down with Scotch and made a feeble attempt to slash through the veins on his left wrist. The police whisked him off to hospital. He was charged with six counts of murder. As Crown Prosecutor Wendy Robinson QC studied the case brief in October 1990, the question that ran through her mind was: 'Where are the rest of them?'

Dennis O'Toole was ahead of her. Glover had killed at least three other women in New South Wales, he was damned sure of that. Two elderly women had been bashed and strangled near the coastal town of Umina in the 1980s, and their killer used a modus operandi that fitted Glover's to a tee. Then there was one other high-profile case that O'Toole became convinced marked John Glover's first murder: Florence Broadhurst.

As far as he could see, there was no direct connection between Glover and Broadhurst but the psychological fit was perfect. Not only did the ferocity and unusual post-mortem posing of the body mirror that of Glover's later victims, but Broadhurst was his type – matriarchal, self-confident and elderly. Glover's name had not come up in the first investigation, so he had never even been questioned about it, but O'Toole felt the similarities were too striking to go past.

'Florence was the first,' O'Toole says, 'Certainly from our investigations. We went very close to charging John Glover on "evidence of similar facts", which you could do in those days, but the prosecution were going to put all sorts of obstacles up to it and the trial probably would have lasted anything up to twelve months. The DPP took the commonsense way out of it and we did not proceed.'

Frustrated but resigned to the logic of the decision, O'Toole watched John Glover convicted of six counts of murder and given a life sentence that truly meant life. At the trial's conclusion in 1991, Justice James Wood told Glover and the rest of the court: 'This is a case where the prisoner will never be released.' It's over, thought O'Toole with grim satisfaction. Case closed.

But Florence Broadhurst would not lie still. In 1992, Sydney journalist Miranda Devine told O'Toole that there was a connection between Broadhurst and John Glover. The pair had actually known each other. O'Toole began interviewing everybody he could find who had been connected with Broadhurst's case, people trying to cope with the fall-out of John Glover's actions even though their only crime had been to know him. Leonie Naylor, at whose wedding Broadhurst had met John Glover, was divorced. Her ex-husband, Clifford, had moved away to the Cook Islands. Others connected to the killer were in the process of changing their names to distance themselves from him yet further. All were happy to help O'Toole try to get some answers for families still suffering.

As he talked to people about the eccentric Broadhurst, it occurred to O'Toole that she and Glover shared certain traits. Glover, too, had changed his name and adopted a different persona. When he moved from England to Australia he changed his name from John Walter Glover to John Wayne Glover, sending photographs of himself looking like a character from the Wild West. 'I remember one member of [his] family saying to me that they drew to each other like magnets because they were both the same, both ... not really what they pretended to be.'

"PALMS" R-234"

"PALMS" R-234"

O'Toole asked Glover's wife what she knew about their relationship. 'I said, "Was John ever at [Florence Broadhurst's] premises? Did he know her?" and she said: "Oh yes, we bought some curtains there. John picked the pattern, went to the Paddington address and chose the curtains. We had them in our house for a number of years. They are the ones we've only just replaced".'

O'Toole started visiting Glover in jail. How well did he know Broadhurst? How many times he had met her? When was the last time they spoke? 'I put the facts to Glover and he denied them,' says O'Toole with a shake of the head. 'He said: "No. No. I never met her" but … it was obvious that he had.'

The detective went back over the facts. Family members had seen them talking to each other, he told Glover. How could he deny it? 'He would come around a bit but it was so insignificant it had escaped his memory, he'd forgotten.' O'Toole had talked to Glover almost every day for the course of two months before his trial and was not buying it. 'During the course of other enquiries he had a brilliant memory,' he says. 'Plus we had the facts. From our point of view as investigators, he knew Florence, he had met Florence and he had been to the premises.' With each statement, O'Toole slams his hand down onto his polished dining-room table. 'And there he was denying it. If he'd have said: "Yes I did know her, we bought curtains off her, I didn't murder her", that would have made some sense. But to deny it all. Well, I don't believe in coincidences in these sorts of things.'

Thus began an extraordinary mind game between the policeman and the multiple murderer. As the years went by, O'Toole continued to question the jocular, relaxed John Glover about Broadhurst and the other unsolved cases in the hope that Glover might finally shed light on what had really happened. Time and time again, when asked about each murder, Glover would shake his head and refused to discuss them. He kept up the denials on other fronts. Florence Broadhurst had her rings stolen, items which were never recovered. Perhaps the

Palms [opposite] is an imposing, dramatic take on traditional, vertically striped wallpaper designs.

207

COURTESY SIGNATURE PRINTS

killer had kept them as trophies, police reasoned. Each of Glover's proven victims were missing underwear but Glover refused to admit he had taken anything. 'They are trophies,' says O'Toole. 'It comes back psychologically to Glover and his profile. He won't accept that he is a serial murderer. He won't accept that he is a classic serial murderer.'

Victorian police wanted to quiz him about two other unsolved cases that took place in the 1960s but Glover refused to talk to anyone except O'Toole, who agreed to go in on the Victorian investigators' behalf. He showed Glover a map of the city and said, 'I don't know Melbourne ... where did you live?' Glover drew a cross on the map, 'I lived there.'

The spot meant nothing to O'Toole, who carried on with the conversation. 'At the end of the day I [discussed] with the homicide blokes from Victoria what the answers were to the questions I had asked him and showed them the map. They looked at it, looked at each other and said: "No he didn't live there. That is where a murder was." Glover was playing silly games.'

Before he retired from the force in 2001, the Central Coast detective made an uneasy bargain with the killer. 'We had an agreement that if he ever found the key to the dark part of his mind, he would let me know. If he could unlock it. That's the only time I shook hands with him.' O'Toole walked away. But he couldn't stay away. By 2005, he was starting to miss the challenge that Glover posed, and as the year progressed, he resumed their meetings in Lithgow's maximum security jail.

On Monday 29 August, they met for the last time. Glover had been on suicide watch since May but seemed in relatively good spirits, and wanted to know which unsolved deaths O'Toole was interested in. 'John, we've gone through this over and over in the last twelve years,' the exasperated former policeman replied.

'How many do you think I've done?' Glover fired back. 'You tell me,' said O'Toole. And on, in circles, it went. John Glover gave O'Toole

Japanese Floral printed on silver Mylar.

208

a pencil sketch he had spent all night drawing of a well-known property with pine trees in front of it. 'Those pine trees are very significant,' he told him. 'Have a look and tell me what you see.'

Glover insisted the retired detective take the drawing with him. 'It worried me,' he says. 'I couldn't see anything in it.' He showed the sketch to a television producer who was making a documentary on John Glover. He looked at it, looked back at O'Toole and asked him how many people he believed Glover had killed. 'I said certainly we have charged him with six in New South Wales and I believe there are another three … that makes nine.' He said, 'That's what it is. The figure nine is in that pine tree.' O'Toole gazed down at the sketch. Sure enough, John Glover had hidden a '9' in the landscape. 'So at least I got the satisfaction of knowing that we were right.'

Pagoda [above] – intricate and interlocking.

COURTESY SIGNATURE PRINTS

209

The following week, Glover asked his prison governor to pass another message to O'Toole about somebody O'Toole was meeting. O'Toole got the governor to relay a reply. 'I was looking forward to seeing him again.' It was not to be. At 1.25 pm on Friday 9 September, the Granny Killer was found dead hanging from a noose attached to a shower fitting in his cell.

'I don't believe he meant to do it,' says O'Toole. 'He was setting himself up for a sympathy vote and it went too far.'

Broadhurst's case is one of 400 being reassessed by the New South Wales Homicide Squad's cold case unit but there has been no progress because detectives cannot find the physical evidence collected at the time. Says Detective Inspector Rob Jarrett: 'I can't say categorically we don't have it, but we don't know where it is.' Glover was a suspect but there is no evidence that connects him directly to Broadhurst's death, says Jarrett, adding that without an admission of guilt, there is nothing they can do.

Leonie Naylor refuses to believe Glover had anything to do with it. Her boss employed many itinerant workers, Naylor says, including drug addicts and alcoholics and kept no records of who anyone was. Her murderer could have been anybody, she says.

O'Toole says, 'Glover did have the luck of the devil on his side,' citing the two other unsolved murders that he believes might have been linked to Glover using modern forensic techniques, had the evidence not been thrown away. 'A [police] commander, in his wisdom, said, "Oh we don't need all these old exhibits", and he destroyed all the old exhibits, including two of them which were murder scenes … If only we had those exhibits now. Because there was DNA.'

As far as Broadhurst is concerned: 'We are just that little bit short of a gallop. It is the passage of time: witnesses have died, exhibits have been lost … It is very frustrating. [Glover] certainly beat me on this one, and there is no resolution for the family. That was the appeal that I was trying to make to Glover but it fell on deaf ears. I tried. And I failed.'

chapter eight

'Either that wallpaper goes or I do.'

Curtain call

There is no escaping Florence Broadhurst. Inside Signature Prints' unassuming, white-walled factory in the Sydney suburb of Rosebery, a team of printers is busy recreating long-lost designs which are now being sold everywhere from Venezuala to Japan, Croatia and the United States. Beside the printing area lies an art room, the domain of the softly spoken, 57-year-old Huang Chongfu, a Taiwanese artist whose days are spent at a lightbox, hair-thin paintbrush in hand, repairing Broadhurst's artwork. So far, Huang has restored a fraction of her designs back to a useable condition. Asked how much longer it will take him to restore the 500-odd patterns, his face crumples with tired resignation. 'Five years?' he guesses. 'Long time.'

Images alone rarely make people sit up and take notice but word of Florence Broadhurst has spread way beyond the enclosed world of design devotees. As David Lennie puts it: 'Cocooned in the life and times of Florence Broadhurst? Yeah, it's a great story.' As the local cult has grown, half-hearted attempts to link Broadhurst's death with financial scams have emerged, as well as a new series of

Phoenix [opposite], here printed in purple ink on white paper, is Broadhurst's interpretation of the fabulous mythical bird.

COURTESY SIGNATURE PRINTS

rumours easier to repeat than to refute. First there's the one that Lady (Sonia) McMahon, wife of the late Australian prime minister William McMahon and mother of actor Julian McMahon, was a close friend of Broadhurst's and had sought out her advice on decorating. According to Lady McMahon, neither aspect of this statement is true. Broadhurst's face was one of those that popped up at social events but that was it and Lady McMahon never needed wallpaper at the time. 'I wish I had known her better,' she says.

Then there's the rumour that Broadhurst was a good friend of Barry Humphries, reknowned creator of Dame Edna Everage and Sir Les Patterson. 'I think I met Florence,' Humphries responds when questioned about it. 'But my mind is a blank.' Or the notion that Broadhurst had a close relationship with disgraced Sydney businessman Abe Saffron, once described in parliament as one of the principle characters in organised crime in Australia. Saffron says he does not remember Florence Broadhurst at all.

Fingers [opposite], here custom-made before Broadhurst's death for one of her original clients.

Love her or hate her, the reassessment of Broadhurst and her work is not going to stop. In September 2005, when Sydney's Powerhouse Museum opened a permanent new gallery to celebrate the contribution of key individuals to Australian culture and design, the first person showcased was Florence Broadhurst. One big question remains, says senior curator Anne-Marie Van de Ven: 'How much of her work did Florence actually draw?'

The answer is simple. There is no evidence to suggest that Broadhurst drew any of the designs that appear under her name at all. Does this mean that Florence Broadhurst's last great role, her pivotal performance as one of Australia's greatest designers, was a sham? 'Not necessarily,' says Associate Professor Lyndon Anderson of the Faculty of Design at Swinburne University of Technology after hearing how Broadhurst operated. 'There is a well-established tradition of designers not putting pen to paper,' he advises. British pottery maestro Josiah Wedgwood managed to avoid it two centuries ago and London designer Paul Smith shuns it to this day.

'What matters is context and intention,' says Anderson. If somebody is directing artists to produce innovative, aesthetic, repeatable images, they are a designer. 'The idea that a designer has to actually do the drawings for the wallpaper themselves is not the case.'

The measure of Florence Broadhurst's success is simple: it is marked by sales. Under Broadhurst's exacting supervision between 1961 and 1977, a studio of largely untrained but very talented artists produced a unique archive of over 500 designs. They hit on patterns that appealed during Broadhurst's life and continue to appeal today – images that prompt desires of possession. People want to buy them.

Diagonal Plaid's intensity comes from its solid blocks of design.
COURTESY SIGNATURE PRINTS

216

Florence Broadhurst kept a tight rein on who she employed and what they were allowed to do. Only when she had faith in somebody's judgment, such as that demonstrated by Sally Fitzpatrick and John Lang, did she allow them to exercise it. Her eyesight was poor but evidence from her son and those she worked with indicates that she could see outlines clearly when viewed in front of a lightbox. At least one of her artists suspects that she spent time alone, familiarising herself with the designs they were working on.

That Florence Broadhurst's was the guiding hand behind her designs makes sense on other counts. She was the only person who was involved in the business from Day One. Her head printer, David Bond, worked with her for most of her design career but he offered no creative input into the patterns. Few of the artists she employed for any length of time went on to make a name for themselves independently. It would appear they needed Broadhurst behind them.

Sally Fitzpatrick did go on to work as a design consultant in the United States but her mother, the respected artist Dawn Fitzpatrick, believes she could do more with her creative potential. It is the kind of thing a mother would say, she agrees, but if Florence Broadhurst was alive today, she would 'make my daughter get her act together'. What Broadhurst had was a wonderful eye for people, says Dawn Fitzpatrick.

'Frankly, she didn't have the ability to do what she wanted to do but she knew what she wanted. She was quite a brilliant woman.'

For David Lennie, Florence Broadhurst is a bubble that shows no sign of bursting yet. 'There was a time when we thought the whole Broadhurst thing could be in and out in a year. Then we thought three years, then we thought five. Today, I don't think there's a timeline on it.' Lennie gestures to the long racks of upright screens visible in the factory. There are so many that they run the length of the building while the ageing artwork sits rolled up and stored in cupboards until a customer orders its reappearance. Only ten per cent of the Broadhurst designs are in use so far, he says, 'and they make up only five per cent of the Signature range.'

When Lennie bought Signature he acquired an incredible creative haul, including the artistic work of Mercedes Fabrics, Studibaker Fabrics, Linda Jackson Fabrics, Noel Lyons Fabrics and Wallpapers, Hexham Fabrics, Boomwalla Fabrics, Blume Wallpapers, Friezes and Borders, and David Miles Wallpaper and Fabric. 'We have over 10 000 designs which were produced over a sixty-year time span,' he says. 'Our film positive archive cupboard contains the history of design for this part of the world.'

One Broadhurst design about to be resurrected by Akira Isogawa is *Phoenix*, a multi-screen repeating pattern of snow-topped mountains, bonsai-inspired branches and grotesque flowers. Inside this unreal landscape perches a single phoenix, the mythical bird that burns to ashes before it can re-appear reborn. For Robert Lloyd-Lewis, this final rebirth of his mother and her fantastic, kaleidoscopic images is a multi-coloured mirage. He loves the idea that she is finally getting the international acclaim she always desired but it comes, for him, at a very high price. Since agreeing to discuss his mother's life and death, he has had nightmares about her murder; about how the attacker appears to have been left-handed; that he (or she) seems to have been someone his mother knew. That they could be someone Lloyd-Lewis still knows.

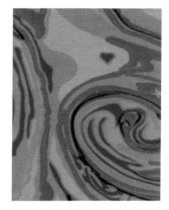

*A sample of the **Water Swirls** fabric writer Colleen McCullough used in her home.*

COURTESY COLLEEN MCCULLOUGH / SIGNATURE PRINTS

217

218 *Chinese Key* – *a geometric design in its own right – is also a 'filler paper', traditionally used underneath a highly dramatic image such as* **Chelsea.**

He can live with some of the mysteries that remain about his mother, including the enduring secret behind her relationship with 'Aunt Dorothy' in Brighton, and he believes he understands now how much both of his parents loved him despite their emotional remoteness. He says he has forgiven his mother for being so eloquent when talking about herself yet so mute on the things that really mattered.

What he cannot come to terms with is that, despite everything, her murder remains unsolved. 'Do we know him?' he wants to know. 'Was it somebody that we employed? All of those questions are still unanswered and it is horrible not knowing. You look at everybody with a degree of suspicion. There must be resolution. That is the thing that I really hope for. Then, and only then, my mother can rest.'

Catalogue of designs

Cover Floral 300

Cover Floral 300

IX Exotic Birds

XII Ikeda

XV Phoenix

XVIII Japanese Bamboo

7 Kabuki

8 Fingers

13 The Cranes

17 Tiger Stripe

20 Romanesque

26 The Cranes

30 Tudor Floral

34 Centrepoint Medallion

38 Florentine Tapestry

40 Hessian

43 Bacchus Tapestry

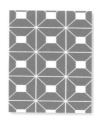

46 Hollow Squares

49 Honeycomb

50 Aubrey

52 Fruit Vine

55 The Egrets

56 Arabian Birds

58 Japanese Floral

61 Pyramids

64 Solar 68 Curly Swirls 71 Horses Stampede 75 Spotted Floral 76 Chinese Floral

78 Japanese Floral 78 Japanese Floral 79 Japanese Floral 80 Swirls 83 Birds of Paradise

85 Chelsea 87 Counterchange 88 Pagoda 91 Circles and Squares 92 Rabbits and Poodles

 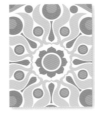   

92 Cats and Mice 93 Pups 95 Small Fern 99 Still Life 102 Turnabouts

105 Khyber 106 Solar 110 Floral Trail 112 Shaboo Bamboo with Slub 113 Slub

114 Aboriginal Rock Art

116 Cockatoos

120 The Egrets

121 Large Trellis Keyline

121 The Egrets

123 Scatter Daisy

124 Japanese Bamboo

125 Japanese Bamboo

129 Yvan's Geometric

130 Spot Daisy

132 The Cranes

132 The Cranes

133 The Cranes

136 Floral 100

143 Tortoiseshell Stripe

144 Roman Soldiers

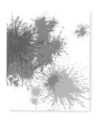
150 Splashes

153 Anemones

157 French Fountain

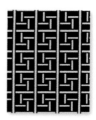
160 Oriental Filigree Reverse

161 Oriental Filigree

163 Crocodile Skin

164 Turnabouts

166 Shadow Floral

167 Spring Floral

171 Milano Tapestry   174 Peacock Feathers   177 Arabian Garden   178 Tortoiseshell Stripe   181 Horses Stampede

183 Fingers   184 The Cranes   185 The Cranes   188 Nagoya   190 Japanese Fans

198 Butterflies   201 Abstract Butterflies   202 Oriental Porcelain   204 Floral 100   206 Palms

208 Japanese Floral   209 Pagoda   212 Phoenix   215 Fingers   216 Diagonal Plaid

217 Water Swirls   218 Chinese Key

Acknowledgements

To Robert and Annie Lloyd-Lewis: a thousand thank yous for your help, support and hospitality during the course of this project, and to that provided by Ben and David Lloyd-Lewis. To Helen and David Lennie: I quite simply cannot thank you enough.

I owe a huge debt of gratitude to Sue Clothier, Nicola Lawrence and Tim Toni for introducing me to Florence, and to everybody who agreed to speak to me, both on and off the record. Thank you Anne-Marie Van de Ven from Sydney's Powerhouse Museum, and all the staff of Signature Prints, especially Catherine Grossman, David Orford and Gabriel Brennan.

The citizens of Mount Perry were fantastically helpful, particularly Pat Smith, without whose work to capture the region's history we would be all the poorer. Antony Barker is another passionate amateur historian generous enough to share his findings about Ralph Sawyer. Thank you to the members of the NSW Police Force, past and present, to Duncan Wise, for allowing us to reprint his family photographs of Mount Perry, and to Leeanne Rose who provided access to her mother Sherdené's work.

Journalists stand on the shoulders of other journalists, and the clippings files we all accumulate behind us. I owe a particularly large debt, however, to Les Kennedy and Mark Whittaker (authors of *Granny Killer*), to Lindsay Simpson and Sandra Harvey (*The Killer Next Door*), to Larry Writer (*Garden of Evil*) and to Natasha Wallace. Information about ocean liners of the 1900s came from *Merchant Fleets* by Duncan Haws, and Natalie V. Robinson identified the Mantón de Manilla which Florence wears on page vi.

Thank you to the wonderful archivists of Sydney's Mitchell Library, Perry Shire Heritage and Tourist Association, State Library of Queensland, Barker College, National Gallery of Australia, Bernardos Australia and Brisbane Cathedral. In the UK, my thanks to the staff of the Surrey History Centre, Chertsey Museum (Doris Neville-Davies, I remain in your debt), Guildhall Library, Brompton Oratory, Churchill Archives Centre, National Portrait Gallery, City of Westminster Archives Centre, London Stock Exchange, University of Sussex Library and Bond Street Association.

Last but by no means least, I must thank Lyn Tranter for being a terrific agent; Keith Austin, Calum Austin and Kathy Marks for their unstinting encouragement; Trisha Garner for her amazing design work; Sam Grimmer for saving the day; and the late great Dr Michael O'Neill, a character who would have given even Florence a run for her money. He will be sorely missed.

Photography credits

All images are courtesy Signature Prints, with the exception of the following:

Photograph courtesy Funkis: 193. Photographs courtesy Trisha Garner: 94, 114. Photographs courtesy Sam Grimmer: 43, 56, 76, 104, 122, 130, 150, 153, 157, 201. Fabric and photograph courtesy Akira Isogawa: 188–9. Photograph courtesy Katherine: 193. Photographs courtesy Robert Lloyd-Lewis/Wagner Photography: xi, 44, 48, 53, 96, 119, 141. Photograph courtesy Colleen McCullough/Signature Prints: 163, 217. Photographs courtesy Mitchell Library, State Library of New South Wales: 11, 14, 18, 22, 29 (both), 36, 126, 138, 149, 154, 169. Florence Broadhurst photographs: Collection: Powerhouse Museum, Sydney: vi, 15, 16, 19, 33. Florence Broadhurst wallpapers: Collection: Powerhouse Museum, Sydney. Photographs by Jean-François Lanzarone: 80, 223 (*Swirls*); 87, 223 (*Counterchange*); 110, 223 (*Floral Trail*); 215, 225 (*Fingers*). Photograph of pink room courtesy Greg Natale; photograph by Anson Smart: 193. Photograph of black and grey room courtesy Greg Natale; photograph by Matt Lee: 194. Photographs courtesy Duncan Wise: 3, 4, 57. Photograph courtesy the Zaishu Project, www.zaishu.com: 193.

Hardie Grant Books has made every effort to acknowledge the copyright holders whose photographs are contained within this book. We apologise in advance for any unintentional omissions or errors and will be pleased to insert the appropriate acknowledgement to any companies or individuals in any subsequent edition of this book.

Index

227

229